GOODBYE, PET

ALSO BY BEL MOONEY

GOODBYE, PET & SEE YOU IN HEAVEN

A Memoir of Animals, Love and Loss

BEL MOONEY

Biteback Publishing

This edition published in Great Britain in 2017 by
Biteback Publishing Ltd
Westminster Tower
3 Albert Embankment
London SE1 7SP
Copyright © Bel Mooney 2016, 2017

ISBN 978-1-78590-233-8

10 9 8 7 6 5 4 3 2 1

A CIP catalogue record for this book is available from the British Library.

Set in Goudy by Adrian McLaughlin

Printed and bound in Great Britain by
CPI Group (UK) Ltd, Croydon CR0 4YY

For Robin

As the traveller who has lost his way throws his reins
on his horse's neck and trusts to the instinct of the animal
to find his road, so must we do with the divine
animal who carries us through this world.
For if … we can stimulate this instinct,
new passages are opened for us into nature …
and metamorphosis is possible.

FROM 'THE POET' BY RALPH WALDO EMERSON

Do you remember when we met?
That's the day
I knew you were my pet.
I wanna tell you
How much I love you.

FROM 'SEA OF LOVE' BY PHIL PHILLIPS AND GEORGE KOURY

CHAPTER ONE

She might have had months left of her dog-years,
but to be who? She'd grown light as a nest
and spent the whole day under her long ears
listening to the bad radio in her breast.

<small>From 'Mercies' by Don Paterson (b. 1963)</small>

I F YOU ARE wise, you prepare for a long time. After about nine years not a day passed without the awareness chiming, like the sound of a small brass bell in an Eastern temple.

Ping … just there, at the edge of the imagination.

The tiny alarm that warns, 'It is coming…'

But certainly not a passing bell… not yet.

Ping … just a reminder that the lifespan of a dog or a cat is very short and therefore you must prepare for its end. The more you love your pet, the more you must make ready, like taking out an insurance policy. Our beloved Maltese dog, Bonnie, would soon die. This is the law of the universe.

So I would make my husband consider where we might bury her when the time came, even though this was an act of cruelty to a man who cannot bear harsh realities. His face would shut down; if he were a child he would have stuck his fingers in his ears. But I was relentless:

A grave in the walled garden?

No, he said, it would become waterlogged in winter, with the river so near, and 'I wouldn't want her to be cold.'

A grave by the wooden bench at the top of the garden, where we enjoy the last evening sunlight?

Maybe. 'She'd be with us while we have an evening drink.'

A grave near our Buddhist statue of Kwan Yin, in her gazebo?

Possibly, because then (I thought) Bonnie would be looked after by the goddess of compassion.

These are not conversations anyone wishes to have, yet I told him stoutly that I had to get both of us ready, because we must all prepare for loss. All of us. You and me both. How confident I was (after many years of writing and broadcasting about bereavement and an advice column as well, not to mention six novels that all deal in different ways with loss) that I knew what I was doing. That I could analyse my own feelings in a mature way…

Ah, how the mighty fall!

When the time came I felt weak, helpless, bewildered. Of course, my little dog's death, a couple of months before her fourteenth birthday, was not a shock. Of course I knew it had to be approaching because her heart had begun to murmur small protests at the length of days. The young vet nodded with grave sympathy when I said (using my wise, steady 'public' voice), 'I do know that I'm having to face up to the end of her life.' Surely I must have been *ready*.

But no. I shuddered in disbelief, like a vehicle rammed sideways in an unexpected accident. A whiplash to the spirit. This one small death pushed me out of my safety net and on to a murky path I did not recognise. It took a month of grief before I began to realise that, yet again, my funny little animal companion was teaching me lessons far greater than the sum of her (very) small parts. Our journey together would continue, even though one of us would be invisible.

🐾 🐾 🐾 🐾

Let me step back, to when she was a baby and life was steady, or so I thought. Bonnie was abandoned in Bath in June 2002. She had been left tied to a tree in a park by persons unknown, picked up and taken to the RSPCA Cats' and Dogs' Home. Who would do that to an elegant little six-month-old Maltese pup? Fertile bitches are valuable, after all. I used to imagine her watching the cruel person walk away, trying to follow until she almost choked…

No wonder she hated being left alone. I used to torture myself with 'what-ifs' – for example, she could have been used as a football by drunken young men high on drugs and savagery. Such things happen.

But from the moment I collected her on 20 June (which happened to be my mother's seventy-eighth birthday) we would never leave each other ever again, apart from holidays when she stayed with my family. Oh, she was lucky to have been tied to that tree – and I was lucky to give her the best home a dog could have. She was only a silly little chalky squiggle on the blackboard of the world, but she wrote large lessons in love.

I'd never been a dog lover. In 1994 it had taken me many months to decide to get my first husband a Labrador (Billie) for his fiftieth birthday and then a Border collie (Sam) one year later. You need to think carefully about giving a home to any animal; too many people are criminally irresponsible or just plain stupid – as the rescue homes bear unfortunate witness. I took good care of Billie and Sam and liked them a lot, just as I was fond of our four cats, Django, Louis, Ella and Domino. It was my whim to call all the pets after musicians: respectively, Holiday, Cooke, Reinhardt, Armstrong, Fitzgerald, and Fats. Now the tiny white dog was named for one of my favourite singers, Bonnie Raitt – although a red setter would have been a more fitting animal for that great country-rock star.

But taking good care of an animal is not the same as loving it. I had thought I loved Louis, a Burmilla, but realised (once Bonnie arrived) that while I admired his beauty and was fondest of him among the pack, that wasn't quite enough. All the pets delighted me, especially when the four cats and now three dogs followed me all the way through our small wood on a summer evening walk, as if I were the Pied Piper. But Bonnie made me realise I had never *loved* an animal before. This woman who had rarely adored a man at first sight, and who always liked to be in control of events, fell in accidental love with a small white dog. And that powerful emotion moved me on, like a ratchet, never to go back. Bonnie transformed me into a dog lover.

She came to live on a beautiful hilltop farm just

outside Bath's city boundary, with assorted horses, sheep and cows. All were rather fascinated by the petite pooch – especially the sheep, since there was something of the lamb about her. My husband and adult children all liked her and life seemed perfect. But when, exactly a year later, my marriage began to unravel after thirty-five years, Bonnie became more than a pet; she was my chief comforter. The abandoned creature I had rescued now held out her paws and rescued me, the abandoned human. I had given her what they call a 'forever home' but now all my own certainties of 'forever' were collapsing like playing cards around my head. I cried into her fluffy coat, and – alone at night – reached out my hand and found, in the tiny bundle of warmth, solace out of all proportion to her size. She was always on the same spot in the bed and I whispered to her in the darkness on those long, hot, sleepless nights, knowing she was listening.

Animals are faithful. Humans are not. Although she too missed the man who was unquestionably leader of the pack – she was *mine*. 'It's just you and me against the world,' I told her and those jet-black button eyes looked back at me with an intelligence that understood every word. And reassured me that, yes, she would walk with me all the way through the valley of sadness until we both came out the other side. She was there when I packed boxes, when I left our hilltop home, when I said goodbye to all the other pets (who would remain with my soon-to-be ex-husband), when I walked through the door of my own new house in the city, where buses ran past the door. She watched me arrange my books on new bookshelves and unpack crockery in a strange kitchen. This constant little dog was for life.

I detest the term 'handbag dog'. My Bonnie was rough and tough and thought she was huge. She ran with the big dogs and got as muddy as they. Soft and clingy (to me) as she certainly was, she'd yap up a storm to keep enemies away. Sometimes in the street she'd take on a much bigger dog – tiny back legs splayed aggressively, needle teeth bared, 'bark' certainly more powerful than her small bite could ever be. She always made people smile, no matter who they were. Her role in life was to spread happiness.

But it was also to give me ideas. I wrote occasional

articles about her exploits. Then one day in 2004, alone in the new home, I was thinking I must return to writing children's books, since my 'Kitty' series had been such a success. But what to write? I flexed my bare foot under my desk – and it encountered a soft doggy coat. In that second, the first of my 'Bonnie' books came into my head: *Big Dog Bonnie*, about a silly little white dog from a rescue home who goes on to raise the spirits of the whole family in the aftermath of separation. I would not have written these books had I not been through that experience myself and known the consolation of a pet. Five more titles followed (*Brave Dog Bonnie*, *Best Dog…* etc.) and I visited primary schools and literature festivals with her, reading to children and answering their questions about books and pets. Afterwards Bonnie would sit on my knee, and we had a special stamp of her paw print made, so she could 'sign' the books too. Naturally children were delighted. In our home city, Bath, they would call her name in the street, and I handed them her business card, which said 'You've just met the famous Bonnie' and (on the reverse, for marketing) listed the six Bonnie titles.

She inflicted severe punishment when I had to go out and leave her behind for an hour or two. She couldn't bear it, which is why it rarely happened. If I went away for work my parents looked after her and once my daughter Kitty did too – taking her on the London Underground, which experiment failed when she shivered in terror. My daughter was later somewhat to limit her sympathy for passionate doggy-love when I announced that Bonnie was the only bridesmaid I desired when I remarried in 2008. Who else? Kitty feared that having a dog on a lead as bridesmaid would be seen as ... what? ... *unserious*. Was it appropriate to have a dog in church? I told her that if everybody in the small congregation smiled at the spectacle it would suit me well, because it was my dog's job to amuse onlookers (she really was *very* small) and to make me happy. Besides, the vicar thought it a wonderful idea and told me with approval that St Francis blessed all animals. So Bonnie (decked with a purple feather, collar and lead to match my dress) walked down the aisle with me and then sat on my mother's lap throughout the service.

In the spring of 2010 my first memoir was published – again with Bonnie as inspiration. *A Small Dog Saved My Life* told the story outlined above: how she came into my life and then saw me through dark times of separation and divorce – just as countless people have been helped by their dogs. I told stories about famous owners (from Mary, Queen of Scots and Elizabeth Barrett Browning to Mickey Rourke) who depended on their little dogs too. That book drew to its close with my remarriage, a new job as advice columnist at the *Daily Mail*, and thoughts about the nature of loss. Even then, starting to prepare, I wrote, 'Imagining the death of your beloved pet puts you into training.'

At the end of that memoir I described going with my second husband Robin and Bonnie to view a farmhouse six miles outside Bath. He had moved into *my* house; now it was time for us to find *our* house. I didn't fall in love with the rather ramshackle place but it suited other family needs as well as ours since my son and his girlfriend (later wife) would move into the cottage that came with the property. I wrote:

> *As we stood and looked back at the ancient house, fran-*
> *tically doing sums to see if it might be possible to afford*
> *it, Bonnie leapt through the meadow grass and lapped*
> *from the river that ran through the garden. Her impracti-*
> *cal paws were already muddy; there was a burr stuck to*

her ear. The lapdog with the jewelled collar looked in her
element at the thrilling prospect of coming full circle, and
being a country dog again.

So we moved. And now I write this, six years later, in the
home which feels so empty without the little muse whose
spirit still fills my study. And the sitting room. And the
window seat. And the bedroom. She is still everywhere.

Life is so short; loving is long.

It is the end of October 2015. Bonnie has grown old.
We used to marvel at her helicopter take-offs – miraculously managing the vertical leap to a sofa at least four
times her height. Now we have to lift and carry her more
and more. She coughs in the night. The vet identifies
a heart murmur and she lies curled on her bed most of
the day, a husk of the dog who once bounded through
long grass, up and over, like a small wave breaking on
the shoreline.

Just like all those who adore and depend on their companion dogs, or cats (or rabbits, or gerbils, or any other

creature you love), I lie awake wondering when the time will come. Then anxiety about her exhaustion and some incontinence forces us to the vet, who suggests a blood test. Something wrong there … enzymes … too much of one, not enough of something else? To be honest I don't take it in. Ignorance can be a refuge. The heart murmur is enough; my own heart is weighed by the anticipation of sorrow.

Very early on Monday 2 November, Robin rises for the long drive to France, leaving Bonnie and me asleep. He has business in the Alpine Savoie region, with no choice but to go because somebody else must be met there. Both of us are helpless before our shared premonition. It should be said that my husband adores this creature just as much as I do. He took her on, with me, his older wife, as well as my adult children, elderly parents (born in 1922 and 1924 respectively), friends, busy career and occasional 'public' role as chair of this or that charitable appeal. He was glad to look after us all, but the small white dog was the cherry on the cake. We made no secret of the fact that she became our child substitute and felt no embarrassment about our 'Mummy' and 'Daddy' labels. This is normal among pet lovers: yes, you can be 'Mummy' to a moggy and 'Daddy' to a Dobermann, and who cares if some people think you silly? After all, this is just another way of adding to all the love in the universe.

As simple as that.

But for a couple who might feel wistful that they could not have a family together, the four-legged creature is all the more like a baby. Our baby. A permanent puppy (because of her diminutive size) to be doted on with crooning endearments: Rabbit, Squiggy, Baby-dawg, Poupée, Lamby, Fluffy, and more. So silly ... the names we all bestow on lovers and on pets.

Animal lovers embrace their own fond foolery, perhaps because they know (even if subconsciously) that such apparent childishness in fact reflects a wisdom that excludes those outside the 'club'. As a student I was passionate about the poetry and art of William Blake – work that also sits outside the pales of normality, reason, respectability, common sense and order. He published his *Songs of Innocence and of Experience* in 1794, the lyrics in 'Innocence' expressing the vulnerable lightness of the child, and those in 'Experience' bringing inescapable knowledge of sin, exploitation, pain, loss and death. Children are symbols of innocence, of course, and so is

the Lamb, but both are finite, because the world of experience cannot be avoided, no more than death itself.
But Blake believed that afterwards there came another
state – that of higher innocence. I can still remember the
exhilaration I felt at the age of twenty when I learned
this. (Now the idea of higher innocence embraces the
love of an animal to me … but we'll come back to this
at the end.)

That day it seems that Bonnie's symptoms are worse:
the floppiness, the little cough, no appetite, the look in
her eyes, puzzled and pleading. So I take her back to the
vet and leave her, for a test under anaesthetic. Later I
wish she had not been subjected to this, but at the time
you do what seems right. How could I have known this
was the penultimate day of her life? That her stressful
time at the vet was an utter waste of precious hours we
could have spent together? While she is there I take pre-
booked phone calls from radio stations (the BBC and
Radio Europe) – two interviews that force me to focus
on promoting my book *Lifelines* by talking about the vari-
eties of human experience, in life and love. I hear mature,
sensible words coming from my own mouth, but all I can
think about is my poor pet. At this point in time she

is my life and my love – notwithstanding husband, children, grandchildren, parents and dear friends. It is as if my consciousness has dwindled (or perhaps enlarged?) to a tiny white light in the shape of a Maltese dog.

On Tuesday evening she tries some chicken and I send a video to Robin in France. Bonnie is eating! Nine hundred miles away he shares my rejoicing at the first good sign for about five days. Therefore I feel hopeful the next day about administering the medicine. My daughter-in-law Aimee (a dog lover, of course) gently holds her small mouth open while I use the dropper. Bonnie will recover. We will have more time. I know it.

That afternoon I have to go to the dentist for unpleasant root-canal work. My parents have always looked after Bonnie when needed, so are glad to have her dropped off with them, carried in asleep on her soft cushion-bed, pale blue patterned with red roses. My father had a dog called Brownie when he was a small boy in Liverpool; my mother has never been a doggy person. Nevertheless Bonnie is loved equally by them both and has been a cherished companion to my father especially, who found that taking her for walks in the park led him to friendly encounters with strangers. That's what dogs (and surely no other pet – not in the same way) can do. They open us outwards. They bound ahead of us into the hearts of strangers. Dogs have no need of mindfulness meditation, nor Buddhist teachings: they embody unalloyed recep-tiveness and simultaneous generosity. For the moment, for the sensation, for the glory of the 'now' … they *live*.

In the dentist's chair I watch the autumn sky darken. The view from the window is of tall trees, behind the graceful crescents and terraces of the eighteenth century which bring people across the world to this city. The ele-gant room might once have been a parlour, where ladies took tea with guests. For all I know Jane Austen might have visited this very house in The Circus. Now it con-tains state-of-the-art dental equipment – and today hosts a miserable but stoical female, with her mouth open, will-ing her mind to concentrate on the life in those bare trees.

At the start of my hour in the surgery I can see the squirrels clearly in silhouette against the tanzanite sky. They run to and fro along the branches and as I focus on them (to take my mind off what the dentist is doing) it occurs to me that perhaps I am the only human being wit-nessing their activities. That nobody 'knows' them (even briefly) except me. Concentrate. Do not think of teeth, nor Bonnie, but meditate on the life of the grey squirrel. I like these creatures, even though I have heard them dismissed as 'tree rats'. So what? I quite like rats too and it bothers me not a bit when I see one at home. We live in the countryside between Bath and Bristol and since this edge-land is always under threat from developers, I choose to support and celebrate all the wild creatures that inhabit it, even the small brown rat in the drainpipe just outside our kitchen window. They were there before we humans invaded and hopefully will survive when we have gone. Some certainly will; rodents especially have strong survival instincts. Rats and squirrels will rule.

There is such beauty in squirrel movements. Along a branch runs one, undulating like a wave, then stopping suddenly to rear up and sit there, as if the wave froze in its moment of breaking. Then down again, four paws on the crinkly bark, and more of that wavy running, then a small jump across the void to the next branch, tiny claws gripping, making it sway. Oh, little trapeze artiste! Another squirrel echoes these movements above. And another, and another – criss-crossing in their empire. This constant activity, this glorious busyness, is awe-inspiring, if you allow it inside your head. Those small animals know things of which I have no comprehension. Despite my discomfort, and the anxiety about my dog, which nags more deeply than any dental pain, I suddenly feel a huge groundswell of – yes – love for small grey rodents high above Bath, and gratitude that I have been singled out to notice their grace in their natural element. Briefly it banishes dejection.

But the sky darkens rapidly, from the pellucid blue-violet to intense indigo to midnight (at five o'clock on a November afternoon) and soon they have gone, swallowed into night.

(As I shall be, and you, and the pets we love.)

'You did very well,' says the young dentist at last, praising my absolute stillness in his chair. A good patient.

'I was watching squirrels,' I say, and he laughs, as though I made a joke.

At my parents' house, mouth numb and swollen, I ring the doorbell and look glumly through the glazed panels at their familiar hall. Then what feels like a miracle occurs. Their living-room door on the left opens and Bonnie walks to the front door – as she always did, hearing the bell, longing to greet me or both of us, after a night at the theatre, or somewhere else we could not take a dog. So many years of yipping with excitement to see us, and scratching ecstatically at the wood to welcome her humans, but tonight I certainly do not expect it. She has not walked properly for days. But there she is.

My mother follows to open the front door and I gasp with delight as I bend to scoop up my pet.

'Look, she walked to meet me!' I babble. 'How amazing! I'm so thrilled! She must be getting better!'

The dog walked to the front door in response to the bell, as she has for nearly fourteen years. What else can I do but take it as a sign, if not of recovery, of reprieve? The glass is half full; my parents share my elation. 'She likes being in this house,' my mother says.

Shortly afterwards I bid them goodbye. On the passenger seat, curled in her soft blue bed patterned with red roses, Bonnie sleeps. Despite my numb mouth I feel a great sense of calm, a mood probably begun by those squirrels. Nature wraps me round in a comfort-blanket of acceptance, as passing headlights briefly illuminate the interior of my car … *flash, flash, flash,* like moments of insight … along the four-mile road to our home.

Fifteen minutes later I pull up outside the dark house, rush to put on lights, then lift Bonnie out of the car.

Is that a sudden tremor I see? Hard to tell in the darkness. Reassuring her with the usual pet names, I carry her bed from the car and into the breakfast room, bending to put it down in the usual place.

Then she shudders.

I fall to my knees on the stone-flagged floor.

Small shocks shiver through my dog's frail body and I know what is happening. This little life is running out. Her flesh is suffering earth tremors, but her soul is scampering along the branch of a high tree and will soon leap into the air, falling beyond the blue dark, to where I cannot catch her.

Picking up bed and dog in one swift motion I deposit the precious bundle on the red-and-white checked cloth on our kitchen table and drop down into the chair at its end. Then I lean forward to wrap both arms around the bed and squeeze it tight around her, knowing that she can feel herself enveloped in this last maternal hug. My face buried in her white fur, my sobs echo the tremors of her tiny body and I wail, 'Oh, my darling, you must go. You need to rest now. You don't have to stay for me, my Bonnie. You can go. I love you and I'll never forget you. But you must rest…'

These are the last words she will hear – and it will comfort me forever that she died with them in her ears, feeling the strength of my arms. Her tongue is lolling out (as it always did, comically in age, with no front teeth as a barrier) and as the tears stream down my face, something impels me to stroke a forefinger across my cheek, wet it, and tenderly anoint her tongue. Miraculously she pulls it back into her mouth, drawing the last kiss into her body, and then the tiny point of light in her dark eyes dwindles and goes out.

There was a great stillness in the room. 'Bonnie?' I called and thought she heard, even giving her a small shake to be sure. But she was no longer there. Then I telephoned my husband in France and his disbelief echoed my own, because first she had eaten that morsel of chicken and then he placed his faith in medicine, as you do. We had just denied what was inevitable – as people will.

His voice broke up. I said goodbye then ran to tell my daughter-in-law, who was putting her three-year-old to bed in the cottage next door. Barnaby's little face was solemn as he saw his grandmother cry for the first time ever, and could not understand why his mother hugged her, why *her* eyes grew wet too, why there was this change in the air…

I returned to my dog – so silent, so still – but, minutes later, Aimee brought Barnaby down in his pyjamas, explaining that the little boy wanted to *see* Bonnie, wanted to say goodbye. But how can a small child understand the meaning of the diminutive corpse on a blue bed patterned with red roses, lying so strangely on the kitchen table where no dog should be – especially when his own mother bends to put a kiss on the dog's head?

Beyond understanding for me, let alone a child.

I telephoned my daughter – because, after all, a family pet is just that. Kitty, now heavily pregnant, was twenty-two when Bonnie arrived in our lives. The presence of the small white dog was a constant as she graduated, started work, saw her parents separate, left to travel with a friend for six months, came back to celebrate her grandmother's eightieth birthday, courted, got engaged, married, bought a home, moved again further into Bath, chose a large black Labradoodle they called Freddie, had her first child, moved again to be near us in the country, fell pregnant again… Kitty pretended to be irritated by Bonnie's yaps, but was fond of my dog and dreaded the inevitable end.

Now, as he was putting their three-year-old, Chloe, to bed, her husband Ed (who would never have said lap-dogs were his thing) decided that they could not possibly leave me alone, but would come – all three of them plus Freddie – to be with me, bearing supper and champagne.

'We have to toast Bonnie,' Kitty said.

And so we would.

But first, before they arrived, moving like a zombie, I set about preparations to honour my dog. All my life I have loved ritual; this was instinctive. First I photographed her in the blue bed patterned with red roses. Then I found a piece of cardboard about 50 by 30 centimetres, and wrapped around it one of my shawls, patterned in pale green and turquoise, the colours of nature and the spirit. Then I gently lifted Bonnie (still warm, still soft) on to this 'bier' and folded the fabric around her, so that just her head showed. She looked as if she were sleeping on her left side, safe in a rather elegant bed.

Next I carried her into the conservatory/dining room that leads through doors off our kitchen – unheated in winter, unless for a special occasion. On the glass dining table I placed my little dog, and lit a tall double candlestick at her head. Then I set tea lights around her, and one scented candle wafting summer jasmine into the cool room, in defiance of the wintry darkness outside. Finally I photographed her again, from two sides.

The significance of these pictures would only dawn on me months later.

When my son arrived home to the news, he walked down from his house and stood with Bonnie, just thinking and reaching out to her with his good heart, while I went upstairs to wash my face. Then the others arrived, my son-in-law pressed my shoulder in silence, then lifted Chloe to say goodbye to Bonnie. Like her cousin, she looked puzzled, and I wondered if she would remember this moment – with the small dog 'asleep' and the glow of candlelight in the dark room and the scent and the adults solemn because something had happened. When she was in bed at last, Kitty, Ed and I drank a toast to Bonnie and all the happiness she had brought with her – all innocent of cause and effect, as she was, as pets are.

Then they cooked supper for me, and we sat at the kitchen table where she had been, and ate, and Ed and I drank wine, while Kitty did that unconscious stroking of her belly pregnant women do, as if they possess the key to the secret of new life and want to convey its mystery by the smallest, most tender gestures.

And when they had gone to bed I took a last glass of red wine into the conservatory, where the candles still flickered around the small white dog who was just sleeping, I could fancy, breath lifting her white fur beneath the pale shawl, ready to come back. But of course the one black eye I could see was open, fixed, glazed, seeing nothing.

I must have kept that silent vigil, staring at my dog's face, for an hour, growing so cold in that room, as the tea lights went out one by one. At last, rather drunk now, I knew it was time for bed. So I blew out the pillar candles, bent down to press a kiss on her cheek, and whispered, 'Goodnight, my pet – I'll see you in heaven.'

CHAPTER TWO

My little dog is buried at the top of our garden,
and I grieve for him as if he had been my little human child.

<small>JANE WELSH CARLYLE (1801–1866)</small>

WHEN EDITH WHARTON'S last dog died she was devastated. The great Pulitzer Prize-winning novelist who wrote *The Age of Innocence* and *The House of Mirth* and was fearless in her rejection of accepted notions of female behaviour – this formidably intelligent, cosmopolitan woman was plunged into the blackest grief at the loss (in 1937) of her Linky. To make it worse, the terrible decision to have the darling Peke euthanised had been her own. Remembering this, in the immediate aftermath of my own sadness, I reflected that Bonnie and I were fortunate, because she had the best passing a dog could wish for – at home, with me and with no intervention. I had only to imagine her dying at the vet's…

Yes, we were lucky. Hers was a good death.

Not so poor Linky's. On the night of 11 April, when it was over, Wharton imagined she saw her little dog's ghost by her bed. The following day all she could write in her diary was a broken statement: 'Can't remember. Oh, my little dog.' She told a friend, 'I wish she could have outlasted me, for I feel, for the very first time in my life, quite utterly alone and lonely.' At last, on 26 April her diary records a cry of anguish: 'Oh, how shall I get used to not seeing Linky any more?' She became 'tired and depressed', noted down, 'Cannot forget my Linky' – and then, four months to the day after her beloved lapdog was put to sleep, Edith Wharton died of a stroke. She must have known that her great novels would give her immortality, but it is easy to understand why the tired, childless woman of seventy-five had no wish to go on living without what she called 'the heartbeat at my feet'.

When I went to bed alone that first night I was in such distress that I had to rise again quickly, stumble into the bathroom, pick a clean white hand towel, roll and shape it into a lozenge approximating to Bonnie's size, and put it in the middle of the bed. When I turned on to my left side as usual I could feel the small, solid shape of it behind me. It was white and fluffy ... even though there was no heartbeat. Where had the heartbeat gone?

The next morning I woke late to find a mug of (now cold) tea left on my bedside table, and the house empty. The family had already gone. In the night I must have reached for the rolled towel and brought it up to my head, where Bonnie would sometimes sneak. I clutched the towel and wept.

There was nothing to get up for. When you have a pet you have to haul yourself from bed, no matter how exhausted or low you feel, because the animal *must* be fed. That is why dogs and cats are effective therapeutic aids for those who are very sad – as I discovered when living alone after my first husband's departure. You might not bother to wash your hair, clean your teeth or find different clothes from the ones you wore yesterday; you might self-medicate with too much wine; but you cannot ignore the creature who looks up at you piteously or (in the case of a cat) imperiously, requiring breakfast.

On the morning after that last goodbye, Bonnie's absence seemed vast – yet still she called me through the silence of our house. I went down to the conservatory and contemplated her body, in daylight now for the first time. It was a bright morning, not sunny but soft and pearly, as one imagines the gates of heaven. The light glimmered softly on her shawl-shroud; there was a vestige of jasmine in the air. My empty wine glass was still there near her head. I reminded her that I always did drink a little too much.

Because I find it natural nowadays to post news on Facebook, I announced my dog's death in what, ten years earlier, I would never have thought a suitable place. Living the solitary life of a writer in the countryside I have enjoyed the communication with others on Facebook, like-minded and not so like-minded. Now I was soon overwhelmed by the outpouring of sympathy. Hundreds of messages, mostly from people I had never met, saying versions of the same thing: 'A relationship with a dog is one of the most special things a human can experience

– comparable to family affection. They are incredible companions who teach us the meaning of true love.' So it went – over and over again. The good wishes would fill half this book.

Why did I not expect it? Reading all the posts reminded me again of how much I still had to learn. Those who do not love animals cannot possibly understand how people adore their cats and dogs and are therefore ready to express sympathy and share memories of a similar loss, or their dread of the inevitable end ('How will I cope without him?'). It was profoundly moving and I was grateful.

During a recent conversation with the unwilling husband I had suddenly stated that I would like Bonnie to be cremated – thus cutting through all former disagreements about her burial place at one stroke. Some years ago my dearest friend watched her husband bury their Border terrier Bentley in their garden. A couple of years later a developer bought all the surrounding properties, made them an offer they could not refuse, and (after a long, complicated and unpleasant interval) they moved house. Thereafter the cul-de-sac of beautiful, modern homes where they had lived was razed to the ground, in order to put up a cluster of huge, state-of-the-art dwellings that might appeal (for vast sums of money) to footballers and executives and their glossy wives.

So what happened to Bentley's poor bones?

No, surely it is better by far for your pet to be consigned to purifying flames than to be left behind. Anyway, that was my unilateral decision and now I telephoned the local pet crematorium to make an appointment.

'We can take care of her tomorrow,' said the kind lady on the other end of the phone.

But I explained that it could not happen until my husband returned from France. So an appointment was made for five days thence; meanwhile it was now my melancholy task to take care of her body myself. Horrible to fetch the large cardboard box that had once contained a pair of black leather boots, and to place her therein, complete with 'bier' and shawl. Horrible to walk outside to the garage, open the chest freezer and lower her down.

'I'm sorry, my love,' I whispered.

There was nobody around.

Birds sang in the trees, as if in mockery of my misery. How I hated them – *and* the squirrel who hung upside-down on the metal feeder suspended from the bird table. Nasty little scavenger. Yet ... wait ... just the afternoon before I had been watching those squirrels and admiring their mastery of the trees. What's more, each January I give the squirrels a special treat – a secret between them and me. When Christmas and New Year celebrations are over and life is back to normal, I take the bowl of uneaten nuts from the sideboard, put my boots on and walk to the enormous willow that stands next to the river that runs along the bottom of our garden. The gnarled trunk forks into two, like giant arms reaching upwards in a pagan ecstasy of air, earth and water. The centre of the fork forms a natural bowl into which I tip the nuts, saying 'Eat up, you guys' – imagining the squirrels peering down at me and licking their tiny lips. Naturally, all the nuts disappear in no time. I love this little ritual. Happy New Year, squirrel tribe.

(To digress for a moment, the Prince of Wales was once derided because he had let it slip that he talked to his plants – as if this were incontrovertible proof of unforgivable eccentricity. On the contrary: I always saw it as evidence of innate intelligence. Lacking green fingers, I have begged seeds in the greenhouse to thrive... 'Just this once, *please.*' Who would not talk to a plant, a bush, a tree and tell it how beautiful it is? Who has not stood in the shadow of a great oak and given thanks, preferably aloud? Who would not greet a cow or a sheep with a warm hello as you pass the field? Children will do that naturally; it demonstrates higher wisdom when adults do too.)

So now, Bonnie in the freezer, feeling angry, I rebuked myself. Sadness must not be allowed to sour things. The beauty of the natural world is real enough, yet it is also an abstract: something existing above and beyond every single human perception. It has its own spirit – the great Presence beloved of the romantic imagination. As I stood there, consciously dragging myself back from that spurt of dislike for living things, I was accepting that my dog was now a part of that world, even if I could not begin to explain how.

When someone or something (I suppose we have to call an animal a 'thing', not a 'one', since this is not a person) dies it is normal to feel resentful of the life all around. King Lear's anguish echoed in my mind:

Why should a dog, a horse, a rat have life,
And thou no breath at all? Oh, thou'lt come no more,
Never, never, never, never, never.

He resented 'a dog' for having life when his own daughter had been so foully murdered. And there I was resenting all the living creatures I could see and hear (in the absence of any humans) for being alive, when my little dog was consigned to the dark and the cold at the bottom of the chest freezer. Every cell in my body echoed that 'never, never, never, never, never' and I felt lost.

Thus, quite suddenly, the death of one small pet puts you in touch with one of the central mysteries of existence: where are the dead? I *know* you cannot compare the death of a pet with the death of a family member, but as soon as you make that statement the qualifications begin. A beloved dog who gave you unconditional love versus a grumpy, unhappy grandparent who was very old and ready to die? Not so easy. And if somebody lives alone and the beloved pet is the one faithful companion, then – yes – the loss of that pet will be just as enormous as the loss of a child. This point was later made to me, with real feeling, by a middle-aged couple, antique dealers, with no children and three dogs. 'When our last dog died it was terrible,' she said, 'far worse than any human loss either of us has ever experienced.' Some people will bridle at that statement; nevertheless it is true for others.

In any case, it demeans us to set up a league table of grief, placing the neonatal death 'above' the miscarriage, or the loss of a brother as 'worse' than the loss of a cousin, and so on. From time to time I have to make this point to readers of my advice column – if, for example, an abandoned wife compares her grief to that of a bereft wife, and then the angry widows come back and protest, 'No! Our situation is worse!'

In every case, *it depends*.

What's more, it is meaningless to make the anthropocentric assumption that human life is automatically more valuable than animal life. What are we – lords and ladies of the universe? No. I have absolutely no hesitation in counting my small dog's life infinitely more precious than the life of a man who abuses and murders a child – to offer just one extreme example. And if you are mourning the loss of a beautiful cat which knew no other joy than to greet you with purrs and delight your eyes with her grace, then you will know what I mean. You would sacrifice the life of the pitiless human instead, wouldn't you?

There is no savagery as dreadful, as unforgiveable as human savagery. No natural innocence as blessed as animal innocence.

'*Why should the evil ones have life, and thou, my pet, no
breath at all?*'

🐕 🐕 🐕 🐕

'But it was only a dog' is what you dread to hear.
Perhaps, behind your back, people you know will
whisper, 'Honestly, she's making such a fuss about a dead
cat!' Or similar sentiments which express a lack of comprehension. I don't really blame them. I can divide my
life into BB and AB. Before Bonnie I simply did not get
why people so adored their companion animals. After
Bonnie, I spoke their language. That small interpreter
taught me the gift of tongues.

Nevertheless I still felt punished with a small dose
of karma. Because although I had never said or even
thought anything so insensitive on hearing of the death
of somebody's beloved pet, I did not entirely understand
how wild the grief could be. I knew enough to write a
letter of condolence to my friend Sandra when her aged
parrot Carlo died, knowing how she (who lived alone)
would miss his morning greeting. I felt deep compassion
for another friend when she told me she would have to

have one of her cherished dogs euthanised, because he was old and blind and had lost the glorious, athletic life he knew. She could not bear to see that beautiful creature so diminished and therefore knew she would have no choice but to look her magnificent dog in the eyes as the vet arrived to carry out the grim task. Yet it would, after all, be an act of love – as the poet Don Paterson acknowledges, in his beautiful, very personal sonnet, 'Mercies':

> … *and seeing only love there – which, for all*
> *the wolf in her, she knew as well as we did –*
> *she lay back down and let the needle enter.*

Yet for all my understanding, for all that sympathy, I still couldn't predict how I would feel. Do you understand, when you have not experienced? Is there a limit to empathy? Once I knew the pain of losing my pet, I was *flayed*, all feelings exposed on the surface of the skin.

Just a dog. Only an animal.

Don't anybody say that to me.

Two days after her death I was due to attend a charity event – a benefit concert by the jazz singer and pianist

Jamie Cullum, in aid of the Bath International Music Festival. Knowing Robin was going to be in France I had been looking forward to the evening. But not now. I really did not want to go, yet I was determined to force myself. My first rule in life is to be brave at all costs. We must. But I was determined not tell a soul about the dog – principally because I was afraid this small death might be dismissed.

Just a dog.

So no blurting.

Within minutes of my arrival an acquaintance took one look at my face and asked what was wrong. Despite my mask of makeup I clearly had no control over my expression. Then another asked the same question. And another. Each time I told the simple truth and not one person failed to express sympathy. They offered their own stories back to me; one woman told me about their ancient incontinent dog whom they cleaned up after with no complaint; another reminisced about how miserable she felt for months after her cat was killed by a car.

A male friend put his arm around me and said, 'She was such a special little dog.' Another one patted me gently and said, 'We look forward to your Christmas card each year. What will you do now?'

This is something that had already crossed my mind. For nine years Robin and I designed a Christmas card with Bonnie as centre of a carefully thought-out theme: the image and the words equally important. Our friends and colleagues liked and admired the cards. So I replied that we would try to think of something for this, the tenth year – even though the star of the show was no more.

That evening I felt wrapped in human sympathy. Nobody attempted to make light of the death of one very small animal, nor give false comfort. They responded with proper compassion, and this moved me greatly as well as sending a loud signal that my feelings were universal. That night, for the third time, I slept with a rolled towel on the bed and reached for it in the small hours.

Should I be ashamed to confess such weakness? No, I do so because I know how important it is that people are given 'permission' to grieve for a pet. Each day that followed Bonnie's perfect death at home filled me with awe, because I sensed (in my helplessness) that something life-changing had happened. Conscious that I was approaching the fortieth anniversary of the death of my second son, stillborn at full term on 26 November 1975, I felt confused that I should feel this overwhelming grief for my dog.

Were the feelings in any way equivalent?

I still have a single ultrasound scan of that lost baby, who was to have been called Thomas Edward. Written on it in blue biro is my married name and 28/8/75. The quality of scans in those days was poor; you can see none of the details that excite modern mothers, who can discern the sex of their unborn babies, should they wish. No – mine is a smudge surrounded by streaks. A sketchy white oval outline which is his head, obviously, with just smears of white above and below. Such a disappointing image, really.

Yet if I stare hard I can interpret the whole thing as something reminiscent of the Eye of Horus, the ancient Egyptian symbol of protection, worn as a funerary amulet and painted on boats to ensure safe travel. That will do. The sad little snap has been my talisman for a long time.

When, three weeks after Bonnie died, I laid white flowers on Tom's sculptured memorial in our walled garden, I felt overwhelmed with tenderness – for them both: tiny baby and tiny dog. There were no tears at that moment, just an overwhelming sense of *belonging* in the world – of becoming a part of all those who have wept for their losses, whatever form they took.

It is fatuous to make comparisons. For forty years I had remembered the date of the birth-death of my second son, rather as a priestess tended an ancient temple flame. Yet I had never seen or held that baby. All I had was the recollection of a worrying pregnancy, the nightmare memory of that long labour and the terrible, screaming emptiness afterwards. Days when I walked like a zombie, numbed by anti-depressants. Nights when I clutched my two-year-old son's teddy bear. The loneliness when I realised that people did not want to talk to me because they were afraid. Is it that they are terrified they will be consumed by the flames? That hearts will shrivel to a crisp if the furnace door is opened? Even then I could not find it in my heart to blame people for crossing the road. All these memories are clear to me still and will be just as vivid when I die. But all there is to hold is a single scan, treasured for forty years.

Yet Bonnie came into my life at six months and remained with me for nearly fourteen years. Apart from holidays and work trips, we were together. She slept with me when I shared my bed with one husband, cuddled and comforted me when I was alone, and then allowed a second husband into our space. I knew her paws, her ears, her eye stain, her lovely silk whisk of a tail. I spotted flea dirt (easy on a white dog) and combed her silky hair to find, catch and kill the little devils. I knew that, beneath that white coat which turned to sad, greasy rags in the bath, her skin was palest pink, with mottles of grey. I saw how she stiffened as she aged – just as I did. My dog and I grew older together and identified with each other across the species in a way that defies explanation.

I *knew* her. She lived with me and loved me and sustained me and knew me too. My dog and I recognised each other – just as dogs know the scent of another dog.

I did not know my second baby in that way.

Yet that baby put me into training, and (although I did not know it at the time) this loss of Bonnie was the next stage of that very long process. Perhaps that's why there were moments when they became one in my imagination. As if my spirit child had been reincarnated as the small white dog, who came along so unexpectedly, for me to love.

🐕 🐕 🐕 🐕

I love dolls' houses: that miniature world you long to enter, drinking Alice's potion in order to dwindle to doll size, sit on tiny sofas and eat from minuscule plates. A significant exhibition of dolls' houses had arrived in Bath back in May: Liza Antrim's collection of houses of the eighteenth and nineteenth centuries. I was interested to see them, as I am the custodian of a precious doll's house my father made for my daughter Kitty when she was a little girl. My mother created bed-hangings and a baby's cradle. This is now an heirloom that Kitty will one day take home for her own daughter; for the present it sits in my study and my grandchildren play with it there – as I do, when nobody is looking. It pleases me to move the little 'Victorian' family around their domain, and imagine them having misunderstandings and rows like all the people who write to my advice column. But here I can play God; they will always do my bidding.

Life is not like this.

Shamefully, I had allowed months to pass and failed to go to the exhibition at Bath's Georgian town house museum, No 1 Royal Crescent. Always too busy with work and family obligations, I let it slip and slip – until `I realised that 7 November would be the last day. When Bonnie grew ill I had thought it would be a good distraction for me to go and see the miniature worlds. But Bonnie had died just three days earlier; now I wanted to do nothing at all except mope. Yet I decided it would do me good to make myself go and catch the last day of the exhibition.

Driving rain pounded on the windows that Saturday morning. Gusts of wind rattled the old casements and drove water through ill-fitting frames to spatter on deep sills. On such a truly terrible day, I thought miserably, the only sensible course of action would be to stay in bed. Yet which would be more melancholy: to lie there alone in the company of a small, rolled white towel, or to rise, drag on clothes and go out into the weather which was an exact mirror of my mood? My husband would be back from France the following night and I had booked Bonnie's cremation for the Tuesday. Now I had to crawl through the hours until both events. To drive six miles, park the car and get soaked walking across Bath to look at dolls' houses would kill some time.

So I left my silent house and went to the city, wipers struggling to clear rain from the windscreen, water sheeting across the road as it ran off the fields.

I parked in the car park, struggled with my umbrella in wind and rain, and walked doggedly uphill towards Royal Crescent – just stopping at the antique market on the way to tell one of my friendly art dealers about Bonnie. Would I transform myself into the Ancient Mariner, I thought ruefully, plucking at people with my withered hands to tell the sad tale? One look at my unhappy face alerted her and of course she was kind. But once I left her I felt invisible once more.

Onwards then, to No 1, feeling more and more isolated and unhappy, like somebody within a bubble, mouthing *help* at a world that does not see. Soaked too, of course – shaking out the dilapidated umbrella in the museum foyer, and shivering as strands of wet hair dripped down my neck. Yet an epiphany awaited. On this grim morning I was fated to meet a long-dead Maltese dog and be oddly consoled. On this grey day of rattling rain and wind I was to hear a ghostly 'sister' speak to me across 253 years.

The magnificent exhibition was up a flight of modern stairs in the museum's new extension, and spread over two rooms. Into small dark dolls' chambers I shone the torch provided, noticing books, china ornaments, tiny items of pewter kitchenware, and all the wonders of these antique houses. Loving their possessions, I sent warm greetings to all the bisque-head figurines with rosy cheeks. When my children were small I encouraged them to believe that their teddies and dolls were real, because I wanted them always to have one eye on the mystery of things and wonder if objects, seemingly inanimate, might just come alive at night. Soundlessly, therefore, I spoke to the doll families in Liza Antrim's collection, because I could not quell the old suspicion that their stories might enhance my understanding.

The large, green-stuccoed, crenellated house called 'Norfolk Lodge' stood in the middle of the second room, supported on a solid stand. It was commissioned in 1862 by a doctor's wife called Frances Boase, in Penzance, Cornwall, who paid the local carpenter £5 15s. to craft this Victorian mansion – for herself, not for children. There were just four large rooms, two up and two down, which would be closed off when the two hinged 'walls' were shut. Immediately I fell in love with this house, and started my examination in the top left parlour, moving across to the green bedroom, then down to the bottom left-hand dining room (what a red tablecloth!) and lastly scrutinising the kitchen, usually my favourite room in a doll's house.

Just then my eyes were drawn to the right-hand open 'door'. And there, on the fourth green wall of the papered bedroom, was the picture. In a gilt frame was a photograph … of a Maltese dog.

"Toddles."

How uncanny, that likeness. How *right* the slightly hunched posture of a small white lapdog placed in position (just as we did each year for our Christmas card), who does not want to be there, yet loves her mistress too much to disobey and jump down. I recognised it. My Bonnie was in the doll's house!

I caught my breath and pressed my nose against the glass case. This was indeed a real photograph, stuck in a gilt frame hanging from a cord, with something – a name – written in very small copperplate below. Desperate to know the name of this dog, and even half-fearing that uncanny coincidence would reveal 'Bonnie', I squinted, to no avail. Then I remembered that my smartphone could zoom. So I took the picture through the glass and the little dog's name was finally revealed: Toddles.

It may seem strange that something so inconsequential should feel so healing. The sweet, silly name confirmed for me a universal love of dogs, and filled me with an inexpressible delight that banished sadness, for a while, at least. Nowadays we take photographs of our pets all the time, but surely then, in the relatively early days of photography, it was special? So it gave me ridiculous pleasure that in 1862 somebody (and naturally I assumed the owner, Mrs Boase) had stuck a picture of her pet dog in the hugely expensive doll's house she treasured so much. The fact that (as recorded in Liza Antrim's book about her collection) Frances Boase bequeathed Norfolk Lodge to her nieces is surely an indication that she had no children of her own. So perhaps Toddles was her baby substitute. I like to think so.

Confirming again that the love of an animal is shared and 'allowed', this little picture left me strangely elated. I chose to see this surprise sighting of a long-dead Maltese as a 'sign'. Or perhaps 'signpost' would be better, pointing the way. There would be more.

🐕 🐕 🐕 🐕

The next day was Remembrance Sunday. The solemn day of respect, gratitude and on-going sadness had dawned brightly for the last five years, since we moved to this village outside Bath. Just before 11 a.m. the congregation of our parish church (and every other one in the land) made a slow procession outside to the village war memorial in the churchyard, to stand, heads bowed, for the two-minute silence, as the trumpet echoes of the last post died away. Usually I found myself watching how the sunlight throws into relief the carvings on old gravestones, and saying a silent prayer of gratitude that my grandfather, William Mooney, survived the unspeakable carnage of the battles of the Somme and Passchendaele in the First World War, and was then evacuated, severely wounded, from Dunkirk in the Second World War – and lived to hold his great-grandson Daniel (born in 1974).

Today there was no sunshine. The wind was cold and the grey sky suited my mood. I felt embarrassed (to myself) to be thinking about one dead dog, when I should have been reflecting on the millions slaughtered in war. War then ... and war now. The never-ending horror that has afflicted humankind since the first lethal rock was thrown in rage. I was ashamed that the tears in my eyes were for a dog. A *dog*. I even had one of her collars in my handbag.

The trumpet sounded again. The world came back to life. Wreaths were placed beneath the memorial; children went forward with little wooden crosses; slowly people turned to return to the church. But I found I could not move. Waves of panic swept through me. In those minutes I thought about the dead, *all* the dead, and wondered where they are – untold billions of them, caught in a colossal web spread on the loom of time. Where have they gone? Where are the mighty hosts of the dead? Did their heartbeats enter the very soul of the world, becoming one with its molten core? The thought was like being beaten about the head with sheets of flimsy white paper – a relentless, light battering of ghostliness that made me dizzy.

If the soul exists, then where *are* they all? Can they hear the organ begin again and are they singing? I looked up at the grey sky and shivered, imagining every infinitesimal space in the air inhabited by a soul. Souls from the Somme, from Passchendaele, from Waterloo and Borodino and … from all the modern killing fields of the world, all thronging, jostling, screaming a soundless *Why?* – their O-mouths merging into a black hole of universal pain, without end. I heard parents crying for their dead babies too – and I wanted to wail with them, adding to the cacophony of silence. If you allow it (and I had no choice in the matter), the imagination whirls away into the infinite spaces and submits to terror. You realise you know nothing at all. How long does it take for the light from ten billion stars to reach us? Oh, how many dead souls can dance on a single flake of lichen on one gravestone in one country churchyard?

Such questions have been confounding people for centuries. Of course, reason assures the modern mind that after death comes nothing at all. In any case, even if you were to believe in the existence of the soul, there can surely be no room for the souls of dead dogs and cats in the overcrowded world of light.

No space at all.

And yet in those few seconds, as I blinked and composed myself on Remembrance Sunday, I knew that my dog had not left me. She now walked as my invisible companion on this new quest: a journey of the spirit.

CHAPTER THREE

*And why was I so attached so profoundly to this little
mad dog? ... Why have I cried as one cries for a lost friend?
Is it not that the unquenchable tenderness which I feel for
everything that lives ... is a brotherhood of suffering?*

ÉMILE ZOLA (1840–1902)

I T WAS 9 November, the evening before Bonnie's
cremation. Robin was back to share my sadness at last.
We decided we would lift our little pet from her icy
sarcophagus once it grew dark, so that she could lie once
more in state on the dining-room table.

We waited until about 5.45 p.m., then went together to fetch her and took her poor stiff corpse (still wrapped in the shawl on its cardboard bier) from the box. I placed her exactly as she had been on the night of her death, with the candles all around her. Beyond the candles I arranged the handful of cards thoughtful friends had sent. The little display meant so much. Robin was greatly moved. His face wore a stern, set look, as if one crack would open a flood. I had had a few days to get used to the house without her; he had just returned from France and was overcome with sadness at the bowls and the beds which I had yet not managed to put out of sight.

The unheated conservatory/dining room was very cold. We put no lights on; the candles imbued the domestic space with holiness. Outside was black but the candles were mirrored in the darkness. I had asked my son to come down when he arrived home from work, because I always find his presence calming and wanted him to say goodbye. It was about 7 p.m. when he arrived, with his beautiful chocolate Labrador, Dotty, loping gracefully at his heels, as always. He stood quietly facing me, on the opposite side of the glass table where Bonnie lay.

Dotty stood at his side … but then, suddenly, in that still, dark, chilly space, Dan and I witnessed a change in his dog. She peered at the table, sniffed, reared up a little to crane her neck, looked curious, then almost anxious. Agitated. It should be said that Bonnie had been in the cold room just over an hour; therefore – to be blunt – there could not have been any smell. My poor little dog was still like a frozen chicken.

Then it happened. The Labrador wheeled and walked right past her human, purposefully heading all the way around to the opposite side of the table, where I was standing. I hardly noticed the movement – until she was upon me. She stood up on her hind legs, put her paws on my shoulders and kissed me. Yes, she *knew*. She licked my face and my neck and didn't get down but went on cuddling and consoling me.

My son whispered, 'Wow!'

Our eyes met and we smiled, both of us touched and glad to share the witnessing of this instinc-tive response of pure compassion from a dog. Dotty was saying, 'I know your little dog is dead, and I'm so sorry. But I love you!' (lick, lick, lick). She knew what had happened.

'That's just amazing, Mum,' Dan said.

'You *saw*,' I said.

My arms were round his pet, my face buried in her silky head. The dog and I embraced each other, while my son watched. This fine animal instinctively felt sorry for me; she sensed that a great change had happened, that I was very sad. Therefore her spirit flowed into the space my dog had left. It was like a blessing from the animal – and I shall never forget it.

This was the second sign.

*   *   *   *

You might demand to know exactly *what* the dog knew. In fact, she could well have scented death, of course. A dog relies on her sense of smell to interpret her world, in much the same way as people depend on their sight. Although this contrasting world view may be hard to imagine, a dog interprets as much information as you do, but much of this is by smelling an object or animal, rather than by staring at it. Dogs can detect cancer, after all.

So Dotty is a dab hand at identifying scents. As greedy as the rest of her breed, she could locate a snack from any distance. The percentage of the dog's brain that is devoted to analysing smells is actually forty times larger than that of a human. It's been estimated that dogs can identify smells somewhere between 1,000 to 10,000 times better than nasally challenged humans can. So for example, I have five million scent-detecting cells, but a fox terrier has 147 million and a German shepherd 225 million. I'm not sure where a Labrador comes on the smell-scale, but I am forced to admit she might have detected something strange.

Yet why did she come to *me*? We do look after her quite a lot when her human companions are working, and I'm very fond of her indeed – but even the most cynical person would surely be hard put to explain how Dotty picked up on the fact that the funny little white dog who was here when she arrived on the homestead as a puppy, and who remained the same size as she grew tall ... that the other animal was dead. And that she was lying up there on that table. And that she was *my* dog. And that I was so desperately sad. And that therefore I needed comfort. What is the explanation for that?

The people who dismiss grief for a beloved pet are probably the ones who will accuse me of anthropomorphism. It used to be thought laughable that animals might have feelings like humans. Their reactions were thought to be a series of automatic reflexes in response to stimuli in the world around them. It had to be accepted that animals experienced basic feelings like pain, fear and anger (obviously, because those reactions are so easy to see) but if anyone suggested that they shared similar emotions to humans, such as love or grief, they were dismissed as sentimental and deluded.

But in the last thirty years brain-imaging techniques have demonstrated that we humans form our emotions in primitive parts of the brain shared with all mammals. The same neurotransmitter chemicals, such as dopamine and endorphins, are also identical across different species. So if the anatomy, physiology and biochemistry are the same, why should the feeling experienced be any different?

In 2012 the Cambridge Declaration on Consciousness in Non-Human Animals agreed that animals experience moment-to-moment consciousness, just like humans. The key differences between human and animal brains (mainly found in the frontal cortex) enable humans to think and plan but, apart from that, scientists now think that animal consciousness is surprisingly similar to our own. So, yes, they can care for each other in a way that resembles 'love', they may become distressed if a companion is in trouble, and they often display signs of grief after a death.

There are so many anecdotes of wild animals grieving.

Sea-lion mothers wailing as they watch their offspring being eaten by killer whales, dolphins struggling to save the lives of dying infants, then displaying signs of mourning afterwards. Famously, elephants are known to display grief, showing visible distress over the dead bodies of companions and even trying to 'bury' a corpse with brushwood and other plants. Jane Goodall tells the heart-rending story of a young chimpanzee called Flint, who stopped eating, became socially withdrawn and eventually died following the death of his mother. There are many other tales of animal grief in the wild, from wolves to llamas to magpies. Two centuries ago, Charles Darwin believed that monkeys show grief and jealousy as well as pleasure and irritation, but twentieth-century scientists turned their backs on the idea that animals can feel emotion. Only observable behaviour was fit for proper study.

But what if that behaviour clearly indicates extremes of emotion? In an article in *Scientific American* (2013) the anthropologist Professor Barbara J. King tells the story of two pet Siamese cats, Willa and Carson, who lived in Virginia. They were sisters who spent all their time together, even sleeping entwined. After fourteen years Carson developed medical problems and finally died in her sleep while at the vet. When she did not come home Willa 'began to utter an unearthly sound, a sort of wail, and to search the spots she and Carson had favoured together'. The cat remained lethargic for months.

Something of a Facebook addict, I have watched hundreds of videos posted by fellow animal lovers, showing animals interacting with each other with huge affection – and also with grief. They display acute anxiety when separated and sometimes, if an animal companion has died, they will show signs of pining and depression. Some vets suggest that pets should be allowed to view the body of a recently deceased companion, and this may help with some sort of acceptance of the loss.

Barbara J. King writes:

Love in the animal world often entwines with grief in an acute mutuality. Perhaps even more than the degree of social cohesion within a species, it is love between individuals that predicts when grief will be expressed. Can there be any doubt that Willa, a representative of a species (the domestic cat) not known for its social nature, loved her sister Carson, or that, as the sole surviving sister, she suffered grief in the wake of her loss?

I find her analysis profoundly moving: 'From this perspective, we may link grief with love, full stop. That is to say, grief results from love lost.' What's more, citing the work of the animal behaviourist Mark Berkoff, she makes the point that 'we humans … do not fully understand love. But we do not deny its existence – or its power to shape our emotional responses.'

The point is – we cannot possibly *know* what animals feel, no more than we can know, beyond any doubt, that there is no such thing as God. Oh, we can have opinions, but how can they be conclusive? Fanatics are sure of their particular obsession – and their convictions can be lethal. The rest of us struggle along, doubting and wondering and questing. I have always believed, heart, mind and soul, that not-knowing is the noblest manifestation of the human imagination.

Many of us will be familiar with famous stories of animals grieving for their own humans, from Greyfriars Bobby to Hachiko – a Japanese Akita who would wait to greet his owner after work at the same spot near the local train station. When Hachiko's owner died suddenly and failed to show up at the station one day, the dog was distraught. But, even in his grief, Hachiko kept returning to his spot day after day – for nine years, until his death in 1935. No wonder this dog is a national icon in Japan.

Then there is the German shepherd called Capitán, who ran away from his home in Argentina after the death of his owner, Miguel Guzmán, in 2006. About a week later, Guzmán's family found Capitán standing guard at Guzmán's grave after locating the cemetery on his own. When brought home, Capitán again ran away, back to the grave of his former owner. At the time of writing, he continues to stand vigil over his owner's grave and receives provisions from the cemetery staff so he does not need to leave. Hawkeye, a Labrador, responded emotionally to the coffin of his owner, Jon Tumilson, a Navy Seal who was killed in Afghanistan on 6 August 2011 when the CH-47 Chinook he was riding on was downed by a rocket-propelled grenade. On the internet you can find a video of Hawkeye, collapsed on the floor of the church by his owner's coffin, and appearing to shudder and sigh. There are so many similar stories – so can anybody question that dogs feel sorrow?

I know perfectly well that, had I died first, Bonnie would have searched the house endlessly and been unhappy. There was always a small but tragic display of misery each time I went to London for the day. When she saw me getting ready she would fix me with a stare like an electric shock, as if the force of it could stop my plans. (*Pfzzzzzt ... pow!* and there I'd be, prostrate on the floor, hair fizzing from all the volts...) When Robin dropped me at the railway station her black button eyes would be fixed in accusation as I waved goodbye. Stricken, she would mope about all day, looking mournfully at the door, until our ecstatic, wriggling reunion in the car at the end of the day. The love between us was a mad dance of joy, as well as a covenant of mutual care.

I enjoy fondling Dotty's ears and know I take good care of her when my son and his wife have to leave her. It is more than meals on time; 'taking care' requires a dollop of love. She knows what to expect from me. So if I were to guess that the dog feels as much affection for me as I do for her, is it so far-fetched to believe that she (with no tempting biscuit in the offing) was displaying real sympathy for me because (a) she sensed my dog had died, and (b) she understood my sorrow? This too was mutual care.

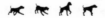

I n February 2014 I was sad to read on Facebook of the death of a very beautiful Yorkshire terrier called Cosmo. His human, Leigh Cowderoy, had engaged with me humorously many times, posting loving messages from her dog to Bonnie on Bonnie's very own Facebook page. Such silliness lifts the day; when you write an advice column in a national newspaper and engage daily with the woes of others, the respite is very welcome.

But Cosmo died of acute renal failure at the age of nine, having battled Cushing's disease for three years. Facebook brought the news, of course, and I was gently surprised that I felt sad for a dog and his 'mummy' – whom I had never met. When I read that they would be travelling up from Devon to a pet crematorium very near my house (at that time I had no idea that it is not always easy to find a good, dedicated pet crematorium in certain parts of England), I decided to go and pay my respects. It did not occur to me that it was actually quite an odd thing to do: one of the pleasing aspects of social media is that you feel you know people you have never actually met. So I put Bonnie in the car, drove to Pucklechurch (10 miles from Bristol), walked into a small garden room, full of strangers, and gazed with sadness at a glossy, conker-brown Yorkie who looked asleep in his box. Bonnie showed no interest whatsoever – no compassion for another dog from her. But then, she did not *know* Cosmo. No matter, Leigh was very pleased that my dog and I had come to honour her beloved pet and I was glad to have shared in the sadness of strangers who no longer deserved that status. There is something very beautiful about proving to somebody else that their animal matters.

So two years later it was our turn. On 10 November we set off for Companions Haven, with Bonnie in the back of the car. We met my daughter Kitty and daughter-in-law Aimee there, and they watched as I laid Bonnie on the green blanket, all ready on the low table. There was already a candle burning in the room (a glorified summer house really, but called a chapel of rest, with suitable respect), but I had brought a couple of tea lights to light each side of my dog. She looked beautiful in her silvery-green shawl-shroud. As I stroked her head it was very hard to comprehend that this would be the last time I would see that dear little face.

Over the years I have answered letters about pet bereavement on my problem page, and believe that many people become 'stuck' in their grief, not only because others do not understand its depth, but perhaps because they do not bother to mark the animal's passing with sufficient ritual. Just reading a poem over the grave when you bury your cat in the garden will suffice: the point is that something has been said and done to indicate that this *death matters*. A child's rabbit or gerbil is very precious; no adult should make light of the loss but should encourage the child to be serious about it. To talk, draw, cry. Ritual is an essential part of human experience and conducting some sort of pet funeral allows the humans who care deeply for that animal to mark the solemn rite of passage from loving the creature who is present to realising that you will continue to love when it is absent. To say aloud that the dog or cat (or even goldfish, if you love that fish) mattered to you and that it will be missed allows you to assimilate the loss and then, gradually, step forward into the next stage of your life.

My husband was too affected to do anything but sit on the sofa and listen while Aimee read a beautiful quotation from Charles Dickens which I had first heard at that other dog funeral: 'And can it be – that in a world so full and busy, the loss of one creature makes a void so wide and deep that nothing but the width and depth of eternity can fill it up?'

My heart cried out, *YES* – and heard all animal lovers shout their agreement. Of course the void is wide.

Then Kitty stood to read a beautiful poem written in 1941 by the American poet Robinson Jeffers (1887–1962), dedicated to an English bulldog called Haig. Bonnie would have no grave, but this poem expressed for me my conviction that her love and loyalty were indestructible.

THE HOUSE DOG'S GRAVE

I've changed my ways a little; I cannot now
Run with you in the evenings along the shore,
Except in a kind of dream; and you, if you dream a moment,
You see me there.

So leave awhile the paw-marks on the front door
Where I used to scratch to go out or in,
And you'd soon open; leave on the kitchen floor
The marks of my drinking-pan.

I cannot lie by your fire as I used to do
On the warm stone,
Nor at the foot of your bed; no, all the nights through
I lie alone.

But your kind thought has laid me less than six feet
Outside your window where firelight so often plays,
And where you sit to read – and I fear often grieving for me –
Every night your lamplight lies on my place.

You, man and woman, live so long, it is hard
To think of you ever dying.
A little dog would get tired, living so long.
I hope that when you are lying

Under the ground like me your lives will appear
As good and joyful as mine.
No, dears, that's too much hope: you are not so well cared for
As I have been.

And never have known the passionate undivided
Fidelities that I knew.
Your minds are perhaps too active, too many-sided.
But to me you were true.

You were never masters, but friends. I was your friend.
I loved you well, and was loved. Deep love endures
To the end and far past the end. If this is my end,
I am not lonely. I am not afraid. I am still yours.

Apparently the tough-minded, solitary Jeffers was criticised because some people thought this poem sentimental. I disagree. He disliked the world of humanity, preferring nature, both animate and inanimate: 'Stones have stood a thousand years.' Jeffers coined the word 'inhumanism' for the belief that humankind is too self-centred and too indifferent to the 'astonishing beauty of things'. Who can argue with that? In one strange poem called 'Vulture' he watches the bird high above him and reflects that 'to be eaten by that beak and become part of him, to share those wings and those eyes' would be 'sublime'. Becoming a part of the bird would be an 'enskyment'. It is a beautiful idea, that we might become part of the whole, no matter by what means. So to me it is not at all surprising that he should identify with, and give voice to, the soul of a dead pet dog, assuring its humans that it will always be there, always loving them, always watching, from its last bed in the soil.

When Kitty had finished her beautiful reading it was my turn to stand and honour Bonnie. Not trusting myself to make a short speech, I just read aloud some of my own words – an extract from my memoir, A *Small Dog Saved My Life*. Concentrating on the page was a way of controlling my feelings. I read:

In the New Testament a remark by Jesus is comforting. He tells his disciples, 'Are not two sparrows sold for a farthing? And one of them shall not fall to the ground without your Father' (Matthew 10.29). So the smallest and most insignificant birds – so cheap you get two for next to nothing – are deemed to be so worthy of attention that the most powerful Being in the universe will notice the death of just one of them. With that in mind I see no reason why a person should not conduct a burial ritual for a mourned pet, perhaps using words from St Francis of Assisi, patron saint of ecology and of animals. He believed that we are all one, inter-related Creation, and all – from the smallest insect to the most noble human being, encompassed within the love of the Creator. On his feast day, 4 October, some Catholic and other Christian churches all over the world hold services

where animals are blessed. Therefore, if the living creatures can be blessed, why not the dead? For it is a short
step from such an honouring of valued animals, to feeling that – since we know that dogs too have the capacity
to 'love' (the human concept must serve) and since one
idea of heaven is a state of pure love – there could be a
spiritual dimension to our pet dogs about which we know
nothing. In truth, I suspect this is not the case, but what
does it matter, if believing gives comfort?

Myself, I lean towards the words of wisdom which ema-
nate from my statue of Kwan Yin, in her garden temple.
She is telling me that we must understand that every single
thing is in a state of flux; therefore struggling against it
is a waste of spirit-energy. Sad we may feel – yet learning to be at peace with a loss begins with understanding
that we must live in the moment, knowing that more
moments will follow, each one begging to be experienced
fully. Clinging to a grief traps the one grieving – and
the one grieved for. It is no memorial to a person – or a
beloved pet – to be rendered incapable of living because
they have gone. Death is just one ending. If it is true that
'what will survive of us is love' then the only way to prove
that is to live.

The girls left. Robin and I each gave our dog a last kiss. Her familiar doggy smell was faint, hardly there, if at all, but I still imagined it and breathed it in for the last time – as if I could inhale her to make her part of me, as Jeffers had fantasised about becoming part of the vulture.

Be a part of me forever, little dog. Shine on my horizon … enskyed … little Dog Star.

Then we walked away, leaving her to be taken care of by Kelly Pawsey, owner of the pet crematorium.

Giving her up to the flames.

Around 1853 Giuseppe Verdi (whose operas have always thrilled me more than any others) bought a Maltese dog for his mistress (later wife), Giuseppina Strepponi, perhaps anticipating the long hours she would be left alone at their villa in Sant'Agata, a village in the province of Piacenza in northern Italy. The former soprano idolised the little dog, who followed her everywhere and slept on her bed. But in August 1862 Verdi wrote to the conductor Angelo Mariani:

> *A very great misfortune for me has struck us and made us suffer atrociously. Loulou, poor Loulou is dead! Poor creature! The true friend, the faithful inseparable companion of almost six years of life! So affectionate! So beautiful! Poor Loulou. It is difficult to describe the sorrow of Peppina but you can imagine it … in my house there is desolation.*

Giuseppina and Giuseppe Verdi buried the 'faithful and charming' Maltese under a willow in their garden – and visitors to what is now called the Villa Verdi can visit the handsome stone memorial by the lake, inscribed '*Alla memoria d'un vero amico*', and see an oval portrait of the blue-ribboned dog, still hanging in Giuseppina's room.

I find it easy to imagine Guiseppina's grief for Loulou, who looked so like my Bonnie, and understand Elizabeth Barrett Browning's terrible grief when her faithful spaniel, Flush, died. Loulou, Flush and Bonnie (and so many others) have a purpose. Because to pause for a moment in the neutral gloom of most days and allow yourself to plug in to the various sorrows of others, past and present, is to be reactivated by an electric current of understanding which can light the world. To acknowledge the power of pet love is to tune into a frequency too high for the normal run of prosaic humans – but perfectly audible to dogs, of course.

That afternoon we returned to Companions Haven to collect Bonnie's ashes. I had not chosen any sort of decorative urn because I had my own plans for Bonnie's remains – and so Kelly handed me a small green parcel, neatly wrapped, and an envelope. We paid for the service and then drove home in silence. I cradled the box on my knee. It was so light.

How hard it is to come to terms with the residue of a life. A small dog's ashes do not amount to much, compared to the greatness of that small heart. When I took the parcel to my special sanctuary in our house, it seemed to me that the whisper of the ashes, shaken in the box, spoke of much more than the end of one animal, no matter how beloved.

That susurration was the sound of loss.

Listen to the sound. You shake it into being in the little toy they give you at four months; you sense it in the waves as you play in the sand and it sings within your treasured shell; you hear it in the train taking somebody you love away; its melancholy afflicts you when a percussion brush sighs across a snare drum; it patters in seed pods as yet another autumn darkens into winter; you identify it with dread in the breath of the sick.

I was miserable to hear it now.

At last I opened the envelope and found some of Bonnie's white hair, snipped into a small plastic bag, as well as her front and back paw prints on a folded sheet of plain white paper.

What shall I do with these things? What do they mean? The pitiful remnants of my dog made me sob, and yet I clung to them, like a medieval worshipper with the relics of a saint.

Once again, torturing myself, I shook the parcelled box containing her ashes.

Is that *it*?

CHAPTER FOUR

For love, that comes wherever life and sense
Are given by God, in thee was most intense;
A chain of heart, a feeling of the mind,
A tender sympathy…

<small>FROM 'TRIBUTE TO THE MEMORY OF THE SAME DOG'</small>
<small>BY WILLIAM WORDSWORTH (1770–1850)</small>

H OW MANY TIMES have I counselled others that it is natural to mourn? Once upon a time I won a prestigious award for writing articles about bereavement in the national press, but all that supposed wisdom fluttered into the flames like a moth – and I knew less than an elephant who bends its head over a dead family member. Years ago the loss of the only set of grandparents I had ever known, ones who played a vital part in my upbringing, did not impinge much (the truth must be told) on my younger callow self. I was sad, but not *this* sad. And all those years of tending the temple flame in honour of my second son now seemed ... not false exactly, of course not. But pretentious, somehow, as if I were enacting a role I helped teach the world to understand – and doing it *well*.

The point is, we are barely 'allowed' to show our grief for humans, let alone animals. Mourning for a beloved pet you feel shocked by the intensity of the feeling yet (after the first days) unable to talk about it. My husband and I walked around each other not talking about it. We love each other and loved our dog and missed her, yet skirted the subject – as jumpy as a postman approaching a house with 'Beware of the Dog' on the gate.

Beware of sadness for the dog.

Beware of the absence of the dog.

Beware of the rending pain of knowing that the damned little dog will never, ever come back.

Every single night (the rolled-up white towel now folded and returned to the shelf) I stretched out my right arm to the space where she always lay, and felt about with my fingers, letting my hand hover about four inches from the duvet, bouncing them on emptiness, concentrating hard, as if that would let me feel silky dog hair. I imagined the *chi* – the energy of the universe – bundling itself into that void and re-forming into Bonnie's own life force, allowing me to feel my dog. This was done with no sound, hardly a breath, because I did not want my husband to know. I mean, reaching out for our dog in the darkness? Talking to her inside my head and willing her furry self to be there? Asking mind and heart to conjure up how she felt?

No, admitting such a thing makes a person look utterly pathetic. Just like secreting one of her collars (the turquoise suede one decorated with silver conchos that I bought in Santa Fe) under my pillow every night.

You don't have to tell me.

And that is precisely why I describe it in such detail here – for I am as weak and vulnerable as anybody else. We are all in this together.

Four days after Bonnie's cremation we went to the

private view of an exhibition at the Beaux Arts Gallery in Bath. The work on show was by a fine artist, Sarah Gillespie, who lives and works in Devon. Her large, detailed charcoals of the natural world are renowned for their miraculous detail, and I dream of possessing one. But this show was of mezzotints and drypoints and, though on a smaller scale, their beauty was equally heartbreaking. A dead bee tumbles through the air like a fallen angel. Two moths – Alder and Ermine – are doomed, naturally. A blackbird, a crow, a coot, a short-tailed field vole, two hares, a moorhen… The melancholy monochrome of all these creatures speaks solemnly of mortality – which felt to me, at this point, the only subject worth writing about, or painting. One mezzotint, a pitiless close-up, is called *My Heart a Wounded Crow*.

This whole exhibition was a requiem mass.

Our good friends Lucy and Tim Newark were there with their son, Max. Many times we took Bonnie to their home and Max loved our dog. Now he crossed the gallery to talk to me, with the gentle confidence of somebody three times his age. At just eleven, he understood completely and did what few adults are willing to do – plunged straight in to acknowledge grief. Usually boys are unwilling to hug their parents' friends – but not this one. His kindness is so sublime it could save the world.

'I was so sad when Mum and Dad told me about Bonnie,' he said.

'I miss her *so* much, Max,' I replied.

'Of course you do,' said the lovely boy with wide-eyed intensity. 'Because a dog is a part of the *family*! You *really, really* love them.'

'Yes, completely,' I agreed, almost in tears.

One of the larger (40 centimetres square) mezzotints hanging nearby had hitherto escaped my attention. As Max wandered off to find his parents, I stood in front of it and recognised that of all the works on show, this was the one. There are no birds, animals or insects in the image – only a dark field, on a winter afternoon, as the last light dwindles to darkness. A wet track heads towards the remaining glow in the sky, reflecting it in the sheen of mud. The tree on the left of the horizon is bare of leaves, like the ones in the distance beyond, and your eye is led towards it by that silvery path. Led towards the last light of the daytime. Or perhaps you are walking away from the trees, from the light in the sky, and heading for night…

Sometimes a work of art will shout until it deafens you, and (if you are an addict as I am) you have to have it. This one called to me even before I looked closely at the title. The work is called *Absence*. It seemed extraordinary that it should be there, so precisely expressing my mood. It evokes a universal experience of loss – and at this point I had no idea whether the walk is towards the light or towards the darkness. I knew only that the path leads somewhere and there is no alternative but to plod along it, knowing that the absence you mourn is permanent. A couple of days later, as if it were meant, I opened a friend's new book and found these lines from a poem by W. S. Merwin:

> *Your absence has gone through me*
> *Like thread through a needle.*
> *Everything I do is stitched with its colour.*

Weeks passed. Robin and I shared our feelings and admitted that we cried when the other was not watching. He told me that he thought he heard her come up to find him in the farmyard, as she always used to when her inner clock told her it was supper time. He would be the one to feed her and dogs are creatures of habit. When high winds blew, the little dog flap (well, cat flap for a tiny dog) would rattle, making each of us imagine for a second that she was coming through.

When your animal companion dies you continue to catch glimpses in the corner of your eye and hear noises so familiar over many years. You can't help it. These are not ghostly sounds and sightings (although many people would disagree with me there), but memories imprinted on the atoms of the home itself, as surely as images upon your own retina. It reminds me of the way dogs (especially small white ones, it should be said) pop up in paintings of the fifteenth and sixteenth centuries: the dog is just there, in the corner of the frame, under the table, waiting eagerly for attention. As they do. As they always have and always will.

I had to review a batch of nature books for the Christmas round-up in the *Daily Mail's* book pages. One stood out: *The Moth Snowstorm* by Michael McCarthy. I wrote: 'This is unquestionably my nature book of the year: an intensely moving and intelligent plea for unquantifiable "Joy" to be counted the most powerful reason for valuing the natural world.' McCarthy, a brilliant writer on the environment, argues that nature has many gifts for us, but perhaps the greatest of them all is joy. As he grieves for the losses (for example, the 'moth snowstorm' on car headlights of his childhood), he offers an intensely lyrical, passionate alternative: the delight we can take in the natural world, in its beauty, in the wonder it can offer us, in the peace it can provide – feelings stemming ultimately from our own links to nature. The implication is that we cannot be fully human if we are separate from it.

The book moved me to tears – closely connected to weeping for my dog. Because reading it made it clearer than ever that to love an animal, to feel such a close identification with that animal's destiny, is to be connected to a natural world that is far greater than the sum of both your parts. Bonnie and I were two rather small creatures – rather like the mouse in a beautiful poem by Edmund Blunden quoted by McCarthy, which 'stays his nibbling, to explore | My eye with his bright eye'. Mouse and poet became one in that instant, as my dog and I were one. As we are *all* one.

The Moth Snowstorm reinforced my instinctive feeling of being a part of a whole: woman and dog, belonging to a great, rich world which included squirrels, moths, birds, mice … all of it. Everything. And that sensation did indeed bring with it a powerful feeling of joy, shot through with sorrow like watered silk. Just as the iridescence of a single butterfly wing flames with all the colours of the spectrum, even as it fades and dies.

I decided at last to write an article about the loss of Bonnie for my newspaper. A month had passed; I felt ready. When you write a very personal column in the press you feel you know your readers, and vice versa. When Bonnie died it was inevitable that I would mention the fact in my *Daily Mail* advice column, but it was too soon for me to write at length. When at last I did (persuaded by one of my editors) I did not plan the article, but wrote at speed. Inevitably I found myself expressing my sense of bewilderment, that question of where she had gone:

> *Many times have I dealt with the issue of pet bereavement in my Saturday advice column – reaching out to readers bereft after the death of a beloved animal. In recent years I realised that everything I wrote was by way of a rehearsal: that inevitably I would have to comfort myself. But I underestimated how hard it would be. The tears come all too easily as I glance down to the space by my desk where she lay snuggled on her bed. My heart aches to know my little love will never come there again...*

In my 2010 memoir I quoted many famous people pole-axed by the death of a dog… And now at last I know how a dog lives on in your own very heartbeat. To me it's hard to imagine an Elysian Fields (worth the name) without dogs, large, small and middling, bounding through the grass – rewarded for their enthusiasm, joyfulness, ever-readiness, absurdity, intelligence, unconditional forgiveness, accept-ance and faithful devotion by sacred permission to romp for ever in the land of the blessed, a perpetual supply of clear water and tasty manna on hand. If this happy picture can console those who are sad, then why not? What do we know of heaven and earth – except that goodness and love are indestructible?

I was overwhelmed by the response. The letters, cards and emails made me howl with fresh sorrow, but in a good way. People sent photographs of their own beloved cats and dogs, and stories about them, and many expressed the conviction that they had 'seen' their dead animals. They all spoke of the comfort their pets had brought them over the years, and described the terrible sadness of loss. I felt *known* by these people and it was a great com-fort, as well as a torture: '*croce delicia*', as Alfredo sings in my favourite opera, *La Traviata* by Verdi. 'Love', he sings, 'is a heartbeat throughout the universe, mysterious, altering, the torment and delight of my heart.'

And that is as good a way as any to sum up the effect an animal can have on your life.

I want to print just two letters to represent the deluge:

Dear Bel

I have just read your moving article about the loss of your beloved friend, Bonnie, and your speculation about an afterlife for dogs and I felt compelled to write to you about what I know to be true, in the hope that it will bring you some measure of comfort and understanding...

I have been present when friends have passed over and in several cases have been honoured to see/hear/feel their release and passing over and to get a sense of their peace when doing so. I have too many incidents to recall and they serve only to reassure me that all of us move on to another existence once this life has ended and the knowledge that the only abiding thing that we take with us, is love.

This brings me to your deep love for your doggy friend. I too, gave my heart and soul to my two best friends, my

Labradors, Ben and Jet. One yellow and a real softie, his litter brother, black and dominant. Both my shadows. They too, gave me sanity and companionship during a (thankfully brief) abusive marriage and the difficult transition into a single life.

They gave me a sense of purpose and a feeling of security. They were my 'go-to' guys to tell all my troubles to, to welcome me home at the end of a working day with nothing but sloppy kisses, thundering tail wags and an almost vocal 'we've really missed you'. They gave my life meaning and over the following years, my love for them only deepened and was as equally matched by their constant reassuring presence. I have many, many glorious memories of them both.

I had to make the heartbreaking decision to put Ben to sleep when he was eleven and succumbing to cancer. The grief I felt was so much more intense than all the pain I'd experienced in my divorce. In this case I was losing something that brought me so much happiness.

His brother and I had to adjust to life without him, but there were times when I would hear and feel a soft breathy sigh and a nudge against my hand and Jet would suddenly look up and come walking over to me, tail wagging, sniff at my hand and then lick it. It was as if he too could sense his brother was nearby.

But three years later, I again had to reach that agonising decision – to part with Jet. He could hardly walk with old age and increasing problems and the vet said he was only hanging on because he couldn't break away from me, so I had to make the call.

My grief plumbed new depths of despair, I felt that my insides had been replaced with lead weight. I left the surgery, went home ... closed the curtains, blocked out the world and cried and cried. I felt I couldn't stop. Heartbroken was the only word for it. I didn't see how I would or could get over this and then something wonderful happened. Jet brought me a gift.

I was lying down, still crying, when I heard a shuffling in the bedroom. I began to sit up when I saw a mist, almost like a softly sparkling fog, approaching me. As I watched, it began to open and through the middle, came Jet. His gorgeous broad head came right up to my face and he put his head down to nuzzle me. I put my hands up to touch him and I could feel his thick fur and I could smell him and he snuffled at my face and gave me a lick. I put my arms around his neck and held on to him tightly, breathing him in, and him feeling so strong and fit again. He came to tell me that no matter what had happened, he would still always be around me and when he knew I understood and felt calm and no longer desolate, he left. He knew how badly I had needed this affirmation.

Several months later, my elderly neighbour who used to live next door to me came into my house for her morning cuppa. I was out in the garden so she walked through the kitchen to see me outside. When I looked up, I saw Jet walking along in front of her, just as he'd done countless times before. She saw the look on my face and asked me what I'd seen but I didn't want to say anything. She then said, 'Tell me – because I've just stepped over Jet who was lying on the kitchen floor and I think I'm seeing things!' So I told her that he was here, visiting his home again. She was so adamant about what she'd seen for herself that this experience changed her own perception of life and death.

All this happened some eighteen years ago now but it still seems as fresh as ever. In fact just recalling this has again brought me to tears. The wounds of their loss in this life lie deep in your heart and revisiting them picks at the scabs. I still miss them terribly each and every day. But there have been a number of times when both Jet and his brother Ben have 'visited' me to reinforce the message that when my time comes, they'll be there, waiting to resume our walks along the beach or through the forests. This gives me enormous comfort. Death itself holds no fear for me and when that time comes I SO look forward to meeting again, my two faithful, loyal, lovely boys, noses in the air catching scent, tails wagging furiously. They have shown me that their spirits too, live on after death, that there is a place on the other side of this life where the love shared between us will be the link that will pull us back together.

I know this will be the truth for you too, Bel. I'm sure from your article, that you are already feeling her presence around you, born out of her strong bond to you. It will give you comfort and you WILL someday be reunited with her. These special bonds we share with animals always seem to come into our lives at the times we most need them to. Perhaps this is one of those lessons we are meant to learn in this Life.

Kind regards, J.

And let us not forget beloved cats:

Dear Bel

I had to write to you when I read your article on your dog Bonnie, it made my heart ache and I have to admit to shedding a few tears. I identified so much with it as I lost my beautiful cat Suzy two years ago. Suzy was a rescue cat. A feisty tortoiseshell not much bigger than a kitten even though she was fully grown. She had already been in two different rescue centres and I was told that she was the cat from hell and definitely not a lap cat! Yet a more loving and devoted cat you could not hope for. I often reminded her that she wasn't a lap cat as she curled up purring in a tight little ball in my lap as I watched TV in the evenings...

She was my constant companion for ten years, just her and me, until she finally succumbed to mammary tumours. She fought valiantly for two years, showing her absolute and indisputable desire to live. Then she went to the vet for a routine op and I got a call telling me that a tumour had finally gone inside her through her lymph node. I would not let them do anything until I got there as I needed to be able to see her one last time and say goodbye. I held her in my arms, still unconscious from her anaesthetic. I do not know if she felt my touch or heard my voice but hope she could. This was not the death I wanted for her. It still kills me to think that she spent her last few hours in a place where she was frightened and having to make the decision as to whether she lived or died in a matter of minutes was horrendous. I couldn't take any longer, it wouldn't have been fair to her to wake her up only to let her go again even though I desperately wanted longer with her. Time to come to terms with it all. My wonderful vet was brilliant and after she was gone he told me that I could stay with her for as long as I needed to. I stayed hours and cried buckets. Eventually the nursing staff had to ask me to go. I have no words to describe how painful parting from my little girl for the last time was knowing that I would never be able to see her or stroke that beautiful coat again.

The flat was so empty without her. So little and yet such a large presence. Coming home from work for the first time after she died knowing she would not be there to greet me, not having her sleep next to me at night or purring on my lap while I watched TV, all these were milestones I had to get through. I still long to pick her up and cuddle her and hear her purr. Oddly it seemed like she was still around for a long time after. Her presence lingering somehow.

Now her ashes are in a box on the windowsill where she used to sit. I have no place to bury them and even if I did I am not anywhere near ready to part with them. Her toys are still in the cupboard in the kitchen where I put them when she died... I have a photograph of her on my iPad and from time to time I talk to it, my last connection to her. Silly, perhaps. Comforting, definitely.

I wonder how long my grieving will go on. I have another cat now, Suki. Another rescue cat, black and white and twice Suzy's size. I love her to bits and would not be without her and have no doubt I will be just as devastated when she dies. Yet still I miss Suzy. Indeed the tears have flowed as I have written this and relived events. Funny, when a person in my life dies, I go numb. I find it hard to cry. My mind unable to process the enormity of what has happened. Or perhaps it simply tries to block out what has happened for a while longer. When my animals die I grieve differently...

Like you I also questioned whether animals go to heaven. As a practising Christian I have thought long

and hard about this. I came to the conclusion that if God
thought that the Garden of Eden was not complete with-
out animals why would heaven be any different? It is
comforting to think of all my cats sitting on the angels'
laps and I like to imagine Suzy getting under God's feet as
she did mine, many times!

Bel, it's never easy to say goodbye to an animal and
there's no rhyme or reason to grieving. We're all different.
But one day you will be able to think about your Bonnie
and remember the great times you had with her and you
will suddenly realise that there is no pain any more.

L.

∗ ∗ ∗ ∗

On 1 December 2015 our second grandson was born.
My brave daughter had endured a very, very tough
time and I was inevitably distraught with worry. The
final stress and danger of the pregnancy and delivery, followed by euphoria at the arrival of the baby boy, took
its toll on me. I have been prone to respiratory problems
since I developed bronchitis when I was a tiny baby, as

1946 turned into 1947, the coldest winter of the twentieth century. Year after year this weakness has laid me low – and, of course, reason tells me this has nothing whatsoever to do with a mother's anxiety or a dog lover's sadness. But on the other hand, when your emotional reserves are depleted your body will succumb to any virus as well as old vulnerability.

And so it was.

A much-anticipated (and needed) week of Christmas parties and art gallery visits in London had to be cancelled. Miserable, wheezy and weak, I could not leave my bed. One day I was lying curled on my left side as usual, too low in mind and body even to read. But the view from the window offered some solace. The sky was grey and bare trees shivered in a light breeze. I have always loved the stark beauty of winter landscapes where the very absence of colour and comfort is an irresistible draw, sucking you into the sombre monochrome of nature's vacuum, like walking into Sarah Gillespie's mezzotint. I could see the gazebo, which forms a temple for my large stone statue of Kwan Yin, at the very edge of the garden. Immediately behind it, the Home Field stretches away from the ha-ha, sweeping down to a natural amphitheatre, beyond which is the river. Since we decided no longer to keep sheep, we rent out the grazing for our neighbours' beautiful horses. So today, as I lay curled up, with a clear view to this field, I was delighted by the grace of two Lipizzaners, moving slowly across the view: exquisite, pallid ghosts in pearly light.

The inner poetic resource (learned by heart when I was young and always a source of support when things are bad) brought lines from Samuel Taylor Coleridge into mind. Weighed down by the albatross he slew for no reason and which the sailors hung around his neck, the Ancient Mariner is cursed – alone with dead men on a becalmed ship. But suddenly he notices the sea creatures, which earlier he had described with loathing as 'slimy things'. Now, in utter despair, he *sees* their beauty for the first time:

> *Beyond the shadow of the ship,*
> *I watched the water-snakes:*
> *They moved in tracks of shining white,*
> *And when they reared, the elfish light*
> *Fell off in hoary flakes.*

Within the shadow of the ship
I watched their rich attire:
Blue, glossy green, and velvet black,
They coiled and swam; and every track
Was a flash of golden fire.

O happy living things! no tongue
Their beauty might declare:
A spring of love gushed from my heart,
And I blessed them unaware:
Sure my kind saint took pity on me,
And I blessed them unaware.

The self-same moment I could pray;
And from my neck so free
The Albatross fell off, and sank
Like lead into the sea.

Suddenly I recalled the moment those horses came to me, as if to give comfort, in the last week of Bonnie's life. On a beautiful day right at the end of October I carried her into the garden. A barred gate leads from there into the Home Field, and an impulse led me to open it, carry her through, and perch on the edge of the flat vehicle trailer my son keeps parked at the side of the field. I have no idea why I did this; I had never done so before. The sun was warm; my little dog was like a white feather, picked up from the ground for luck. Minutes passed; oblivious to the world, huddled over her, my senses narrowed to one focus, I spoke aloud, telling her that she would soon feel better. I promised her that everything would be fine, very soon… *no doubt about it, my Bonnie. Can you hear me? Of course you can! In a few moments we'll go inside and you can try some chicken. But isn't the sun wonderful? Can you feel how warm it is?*

I had not noticed the horses that day. They must have been grazing at the bottom of the field. Suddenly something nudged my upper right arm. I looked up. To my astonishment the pair were there, giants looming, driven by natural curiosity to inspect the strange human holding a white animal, at the edge of 'their' field. Silently they had come across the grass to say hello. How can I convey my surprise, shot through with some alarm, since I have no experience with horses? To see the massive heads bending so low, just inches from mine, to gaze right into their tender eyes, see the sweep of their pinkish-white eyelashes, so close… And now they both pushed at me gently. Rather nervously I reached up a hand to pat one on the forehead, noticing how the hair that looks pure white is actually mottled with soft grey, like snow the day after it has fallen.

'Hello, you two,' I said.

Had I been standing they would have seemed daunting enough, but I was sitting on the edge of a trailer close to the ground, and they towered above me. Ungainly, unbalanced by my dog, I scrambled backwards, standing up, so that now I was their height, and talking all the while. But of course, those beautiful creatures meant me no harm and soon wandered off, having seen what they wanted to see. They were merciful.

Now, six weeks later, I was curled up in bed, observing those animals from a great distance. Just as I watched those squirrels when Bonnie was reaching the very end of her life, now I saw (I mean, truly *saw*) them, peacefully cropping the grass behind the great Chinese goddess of compassion. Miserable and ill, I felt overwhelmed with gratitude and awe at the sight of their magnificent bodies moving in perfect unison, under an ashen sky. Opening the heart to the love of living things – squirrels, horses, dogs – drives out the preoccupations of self. Then, into the gap that remains, all the universe can flow.

Was this an unconscious blessing? It was certainly a feeling akin to love. When you reach out to 'happy living things' with a full heart, miracles can happen.

And so it was.

Bonnie used to sleep on top of the duvet in the middle of the bed, usually pressed up behind me, against the curve of my legs. That was her place. Now, as I watched the horses, I felt her there. A sudden pressure, almost a shove against me. The room seemed to hold its breath. The silence roared – as I felt that little push again. She nudged me. She was present. She was telling me she was there.

I spoke aloud. 'Bonnie…?'

The stillness in the bedroom enfolded us both.

'I know you're here, Bonnie,' I said.

She was.

There was no mistaking the feeling of that little animal mass; for fourteen years I was accustomed to its insistent heft. Of course, even as I write, I know some people will reckon that a sick woman on antibiotics will imagine she feels the presence of her dog. Poor thing!

But recording here what is absolutely true, I rejoice in not caring a mouse's breath what anybody thinks.

There was an unmistakable physicality to that nudging. Bonnie was *there*.

A rational and sophisticated woman, I do not believe in ghosts, despite being permanently alive to 'mystery'. Surely all writers need to keep their imaginations open to myth, to possibility, to things unfathomable? But although it would please me to report (as so many of my readers did, responding to my newspaper article) that I actually saw my beloved pet in the corners of the room – I never did. Nor did I once expect actually to hear or feel her presence, although it was no surprise that I sensed her spirit everywhere. So I dismiss the notion that wishful thinking led to the sudden surprise of that palpable pressure in the small of my back.

Until I die I will cherish this truth: for those few minutes, as I steadfastly stared at the grey-green field and the elegant white horses, I felt the actual, physical presence of my dog in the electric stillness of the bedroom. Frozen, I was incapable of turning around, and within seconds the experience had passed. It never happened again, but it did happen then.

My dog was dead, but she came to me.
I accepted it as the third sign.

CHAPTER FIVE

A stretching cat is a book of wisdom
opening slowly at the right page.

<small>CHRISTIAN BOBIN (B. 1951)</small>

WHAT HAUNTED ME was not one small white dog but what she represented. I sat, books open on my lap, meditating on the little doggy faces (invariably white) you see so often in the corner of the fifteenth- and sixteenth-century pictures I love so much. One in the British Museum, an illustration in *The Book of the Queen*, by Christine de Pizan, shows a lady (presumably the author) at her writing desk, at her feet the small white dog wearing an ornamented collar. When Bonnie died, this image, which used to make me smile in recognition, had the opposite effect.

Why, I wondered, have humans so long cherished this ancient love of the dog – and the inevitable grief at its passing? Does it teach us more than a simple truth about mutual need? At this point I did not want to come to terms with Bonnie's absence, so much as to contemplate it and understand what it meant. Might you call this wallowing in grief? If so, you would be wrong.

Answering problem letters from readers, I very rarely counsel 'moving on', because I dislike that glib phrase that pushes sorrow away. Why should you move on? Better by far to take hold of the feelings, greet them as old friends and get to know them better, allowing them to add to the totality of who you are. They may well change you – in fact, ideally they should. That becomes the next step, and at that point you may call it a move forwards, if you like. But it is not so much a leaving behind as a gathering up. I read once that psychotherapists believe it is not the loss itself but what it uncovers within you that brings despair. But perhaps not if you put it on a lead and take it for a walk.

Anyone who has felt sadness at the loss of a beloved animal will know quite well the nature of the gap. Here is my list, off the top of my head:

1. Friend and anchor
2. Keen playmate
3. Uncritical counsellor
4. Thing of beauty
5. Baby
6. Outdoor companion (in youth, anyway)

7. Entertainer
8. Devoted admirer
9. Ever-grateful recipient of devotion
10. Confessor
11. Muse
12. Anti-depressant

That is a large vacancy to fill. A sinkhole opens in your life and in you slide, wondering how deep this will go. That list of functions or qualities will be recognised by dog lovers for certain, but probably by cat lovers too. As someone who has known both types of companionship, I truly appreciate the strange magic of cats, so different from that of dogs. But all such generalisations are flawed and therefore pointless, since each dog has its own personality, and cats do too. Not just cats and dogs: some rabbits are more aggressive than others, some budgies less talkative ... although I have never met a single hamster (and I knew four when my daughter was small) who did not want desperately, tragically, to escape from petted captivity.

If the shrinks are correct about the sub-text to sadness, what was lurking at the very bottom of my sinkhole?

When a beloved pet dies you also mourn the loss of the person you became during your time together. The animal marked a stage; its death signals loudly that a certain portion of your allotted time is now over, transforming the pet's mortality into a harbinger of your own. When you commit to a relationship with an animal, you inevitably change – because I believe that the process of truly loving *anything* (or anybody) must create a shift in personality. (It should make you better, although the opposite can be the case.) And now that precious time is over, what will be the next catalyst for positive change in your life?

When Bonnie died I looked back with intense, almost unhealthy nostalgia to the summer day when she came to live with me. It was very, very hot and at the time I drove a sports car with a manual roof. I turned up at the RSPCA Cats' and Dogs' Home with no special bag, basket or cage to stow her in, so plonked her on the passenger seat in the sunshine. We looked at each other, both rather nervous. Then I grew worried that she might jump out of the car – which was obviously impossible, since this was not a baby kangaroo, but reveals how inexperienced I was in the matter of small dogs and their ways. So I got out and hauled the heavy hood over us, clunking it tightly shut. With that action I was symbolically creating a haven for the two of us which nobody else (no matter how fond of her) would ever really be able to enter.

I brooded over those days. Rerunning the mental videos of times past opened up the other deep sadness: the loss of the life we all shared. The little white dog had trotted into a settled (if complicated) family in a wonderful old hilltop farmhouse, joining the other animals in the most beautiful environment. Just one year later the whole edifice of Home would shiver, crack, crumble and gradually fall – and just eight years after that the whole house (very old but unlisted), beautiful barn and magnificent outbuildings would themselves be demolished by new owners, in an act of incomprehensible vandalism I still find it impossible to forgive. Yet it was symbolic too: traces of long-standing love imprinted on old stones, now obliterated.

When the tears came into my eyes because Bonnie was no longer with me, I was also crying for all the other things that had gone: that marriage; my children, then still in their teens and early twenties; the summer days when friends sat around the big wooden table on the back terrace; the way my husband and I would stand outside the kitchen door and marvel at how the morning mist obscured the whole valley below us, while we stood in sunshine above, speechless. I was reminded (with some bitterness as well as sorrow) of how much *better* we could have been; how it all might have been saved; how humans mess up their own lives and there seems to be no help for it.

In contrast, my relationship with my dog was the most uncomplicated I had ever enjoyed. When you use the word 'relationship' about an animal, you know those who cannot understand will tut. How can you elevate your affection for the lolloping Labrador who just associates you with food, strokes and walks to the status of *relationship*? How can you claim such mutuality with a cat who stalks into the house with apparently grand indifference? But the man or woman who loves that dog or cat will completely understand. You have to love and be loved by an animal to be admitted into a certain 'club' – not of potty, anthropomorphic animal-loving sentimentalists, but of human beings who happen to understand their role within a greater whole.

(At this point people may quibble at my use of the

word 'love' as well as the word 'relationship'. They will say that an animal cannot know what it means to 'love'. Enough, enough! You must reach the end of this book and then decide…)

Family life has always been my centre. Childhood was centred on a small, tight web of relationships: grandparents, parents, brother, cousins, aunts and uncles: close, boisterous and very ordinary – if that word has any meaning, when I consider certain darker undercurrents I became aware of as I grew older. Once married, I was (unwittingly, and within a very different environment and class) to replicate both the closeness and the complications … but that is another story. The point I want to make here is that even though I love my parents, my children, my first husband, my very close friends and my second husband, all those relationships have seemed, at one stage or another, flawed. People will always disappoint, frustrate and hurt you, just as you know quite well (or at least you should) that you yourself have the capacity to let them down too, unforgivably, from time to time.

But the dog? My dog was flawless. She never disappointed me. She offered a relationship that could not be improved on. Your animal companion's needs are few:

food, shelter, affection, and in return you will receive unstinting fidelity of a quality that can move you to tears. What's more, you know that if your financial and domestic circumstances were to collapse, a dog would willingly follow you into a wind-blasted hovel to huddle with you through the night, bestowing warmth. Within the silence of your pet you find a wealth of fine conversation. In the sympathy of your pet, a world of wisdom. In the devotion of your pet, the most profound consolation. No human, no matter how adored, can equal it.

When Bonnie was dead, I brooded on the fault lines within all my relationships, past and present, and on my own sins and weaknesses. I could have been a much better mother, daughter, wife. I made too-easy career choices that arguably betrayed both my potential and my dreams. To others, I appeared more than I was; to myself, much less. In other words, I was a fraud. Yet Bonnie knew me only as the utterly authentic and perfect mother, carer, friend – and now I had lost that magic mirror that told me what I wanted to hear. No wonder her loss uncovered aching wistfulness. Recently, I had the habit of whispering to her that we two girls were growing old together. Now I had to go on without her.

At one stage in my life I made a point of asserting crassly that I was not 'an animal person' (writing this now, I want to disown that stupid woman). But missing Bonnie so much and thinking too much, I began to find consolation in realising that the seeds for conversion were buried deep, long before she came along. Perhaps my training for loving my dog had begun in childhood. This was an epiphany.

The little girl who was entranced by Rat and Mole and Mr Badger and the insufferable Toad lived in a second-floor, low-rise Liverpool Corporation flat, far from any river bank. The public library shaped me, and I was blessed with aspirational, hard-working parents who fed my love of books. I had classmates from book-free homes, but our small bookcase was stuffed with my father's Readers' Union volumes (Gerald Durrell, Thor Heyerdahl, Somerset Maugham, Nevil Shute and so on) and a fat red dictionary with indents for each letter. I read and reread children's classics like *Little Women* and *Heidi*, but knew none of the boundaries modern publishers impose by labelling books for a certain age. A book was a book:

the story might be real or imagined, but that didn't matter and if I didn't recognise a word in one of Dad's book club editions I looked it up in the dictionary. If I got bored, I stopped. This private world was my consolation for sometimes being bullied in school and for feeling alone within the hurly-burly of my family.

A child like that – skinny, bespectacled, unpopular – might be unreachable. Yet imagination is the saviour, and even in the city flat I could hear the great nature spirit, Pan, piping at the gates of dawn. That odd episode in *The Wind in the Willows* entranced me. When Mr Otter's little boy, Portly, goes missing, Rat and Mole decide to go in search of him and set out on the river at night. As dawn is breaking Rat begins to hear haunting music from a pipe: 'the merry bubble and joy, the thin, clear, happy call...' Mole does not hear it at first, but as they go farther down-river and the dawn becomes lighter, he too picks up the 'heavenly music'. They moor on a little island, go ashore, then comes the moment I remember reading repeatedly – puzzled but captivated by the romance of the words:

> ... *while Nature, flushed with fullness of incredible colour, seemed to hold her breath for the event, he*

*looked in the very eyes of the Friend and Helper; saw
the backwards sweep of the curved horns, gleaming in the
growing daylight ... the long supple hand still holding
the pan-pipes ... last of all, nestling between his very
hooves, sleeping soundly in entire peace and contentment, Mole saw the little, round, podgy, childish form of
the baby otter.*

It is a sacred moment, so full of intolerable joy that the
animals need to be given the gift of forgetfulness, or else
they could never be happy again. As an adult, aware of
the psychedelic shimmer of that strange scene, I can
understand why Pink Floyd (led then by the doomed Syd
Barrett) called their first album *The Piper at the Gates of
Dawn*. And why Van Morrison too was inspired by the
chapter, releasing his track with the same name in 1997
and drawing heavily on Kenneth Grahame's words. His
chorus is 'The wind in the willows and the piper at the
gates of dawn' and words like 'vision' and 'trance' under-
line the pure, transcendental nature of the encounter
between animals and god, as dawn breaks. At the root of
it all is naked longing – for oneness, for wholeness, for the
kind of spiritual insight which changes you permanently.

When I became a teenager I kept a commonplace book and copied out this description of the moment the otter's child wakes from his blissful sleep:

> *In a moment ... his face grew blank and he fell to hunting around in a circle with pleading whine. As a child that has fallen happily asleep in its nurse's arms, and wakes to find itself alone and laid in a strange place ... and runs from room to room, despair growing silently at its heart, even so Portly searched the island and searched, dogged and unwearying, till at last the black moment came for giving up and sitting down and crying bitterly.*

Those who dislike the quasi-mystical religiosity in this odd chapter and long to return to the rollicking exploits of Mr Toad are perhaps fortunate never to have experienced little Portly's intolerable ache for stillness and oneness with the great spirit of Pan. Bonnie's death led me back to my memories, and I realised that nowadays I feel the longing most of the time.

For my tenth birthday (8 October 1956) my parents presented me with three paperbacks: *Men and*

Gods by Rex Warner (a Penguin book), *Ballet Shoes* by Noel Streatfeild and *Tarka the Otter* by Henry Williamson (both Puffins). With my pocket money I bought two of the special kits you could use to transform your pristine paperbacks into pretentious little hardcovers, complete with gold foil you used to write on the spine. How smart I thought they looked! The two (which I still have, sixty years later) chosen for this dubious treatment were Warner's retelling of Ovid's *Metamorphoses* and Williamson's 1927 classic about the life and death of an otter swimming the rivers Torridge and Taw in North Devon.

Tarka and his mother and Greymuzzle and White-tip, not to mention the dreaded killer Deadlock, were all so vivid that when I reached the final, fatal confrontation between otter and hound, I felt I could see the last bubbles rise in the river. How I wept – and hated the brutal huntsmen with their cudgels. Why, I wondered, would anybody want to kill?

When a solitary and thoughtful child is caught up in a great work like *Tarka the Otter*, change happens. You may not know it at the time, but years later you can look back and say, *Yes, it was then*. Although the landscape of the story was utterly alien, I smelt its vegetation, heard its birdsong, knew its skies. My bedroom window overlooked a dual carriageway, glowing orange at night, and its metal frame vibrated when the traffic was heavy. Yet when told to write a poem on any subject for homework I chose 'The Owl' – even though the only place I'd 'heard' one was in the pages of *Tarka*. My poem described leaning out of a wooden 'casement' to look at the moonlight, then hearing the chilling sound of an owl, while 'reigned the mysterious Night'. It contained two lines I still find inexplicable: 'The night had entered through my eyes, | I was bodiless, myself no more…'

It would be many years before I actually experienced what I was writing about – an almost mystical union with nature; nevertheless the seed was there. A child's imagination had leapt forward into the natural world.

My next animal 'guide' was real: a cat. An unwanted black-and-white moggy I called Micky was to hold my paw in the learning process. It was 1961; I was fifteen now, and life had changed. My parents had obtained their first mortgage on a semi-detached house in Trowbridge, Wiltshire. We had no pets, nor was I conscious of needing animal companions. But then I went to a schoolfriend's house and met the kitten. Its siblings had already been found homes but this poor little cat had 'thumbs'. It was a cat with hands. Polydactyly is a congenital abnormality, an extra digit (or more) on each front paw. Sailors thought such cats lucky (extra dexterity for catching rodents), but once upon a time some superstitious folk killed them as witches' familiars. Ernest Hemingway was presented with such a cat by a ship's captain and from then on made a point of breeding and keeping them at his house in Florida. Of course, I knew nothing of this at that time; what mattered was that the kitten with thumbs wasn't wanted (although the family had reluctantly decided to keep it if they had to), therefore I must give it a home.

So I put the kitten into my duffel bag and took it to my parents, lying (I probably summoned up a fake tear) that it was due to be destroyed the following day. My father was soft-hearted, my mother much less so; nevertheless she submitted to emotional blackmail and Micky joined our family. Surviving until long after I had left home for university, he was lucky enough to die of old age and be buried in the small garden of that semi. It was through him that I first learned to appreciate the

glorious, self-contained elegance of cats: their tolerance, their patronising affection, and the liberating knowledge that, ultimately, it would not matter too much to them whether you live or die. I discovered the comfort of a cat settling on your knee, the purrs vibrating through your body and driving away anxiety about family members, exams and boyfriends. But the lesson I also took from Micky was that it is acceptable to be different. Some people will like our odd, superfluous 'thumbs', others will hate them, but there is no choice but to live with imperfection.

I left Trowbridge for two lowly jobs, before taking my place at University College London. Like my boyfriend, I had stayed on at school for one term to apply for Oxford, but having failed to be accepted by St Hilda's to read English, my way of coming to terms with the crushing disappointment was to spend time in the city of my dreams, knowing I would never study there. You could call it self-flagellation.

The mid-1960s was a simpler time with fewer choices, and nobody I knew then took what came to be known as a 'gap year'. Everybody went from grammar school straight to university, college or training (shop management, for example), and although I imagine the children of wealthy parents did travel, I knew nobody like that. My two-term break from education was unusual, but I lacked money and courage, so did nothing exciting. To me it was an adventure to go to Oxford (a whole two hours away from my parents) and, in the same day, find a bedsitting room by means of a postcard-advert pinned up in a shop and a lowly clerical job through what was then called the Labour Exchange. I stayed in that tedious job from January to Easter, counting cheques and sealing envelopes in the Collector of Taxes' office on the Woodstock Road, then moved to a girls' prep school in Buckinghamshire, where I was to perform a strange combination role of kitchen skivvy and nursery assistant. There is nothing more humbling than menial work when you have been one of the bright sparks in your grammar school; you realise that to study is a privilege and yet knowing Latin counts for little in the real world.

My accommodation at the school was in a cottage shared with two teachers. Most evenings, when I had cleared the pupils' supper tables and stashed the dishwashers, I would walk to the kiosk at the other end of the village to telephone my boyfriend, who was working at the Atomic Energy Research Establishment at Harwell, Oxfordshire, before taking up his physics scholarship at Oxford. One night, as I strolled in the mothy, violet light, hearing the murmur of wood pigeons on their way to their nests, I detected a faint cheeping close at hand.

I stopped and looked around. At the edge of the lane, half-hidden in the tattered lower fronds of cow parsley, was a baby bird.

Still a city girl (even though we had lived in small-town Wiltshire for six years), I found the country environment alien. I did not like the silence and was intimidated by the tawny owl's breathless hoots – coldly hesitant, as if he were deciding whether to haunt or to kill. But despite having no idea what to do with a baby bird, I could not leave it there. The moment when you reach forward tentatively to cradle a wild thing in your hand is life-changing – although you have no idea of that at the time. You cannot cherish beauty in a clenched fist.

Tender and afraid, I picked up the fledgling and carried him back to the cottage, feeling acutely responsible for the life of another living being. Recently bought sandals provided an empty shoebox. Torn-up grass and leaves created a soft bed. But what did he need? Milk and water, I thought, not thinking of worms – and even if I had, I doubt I'd have had the will to find them. I called him Fred and for three days kept him alive on minute pellets of bread soaked in warm milk, held out on a fingertip.

my fred.
July 1966.

Was this the right thing to do? I have no idea. I only
know that I was thrilled that his eyes were bright, that
his cheep sounded stronger, that he appeared to be gaining strength. I lifted the baby from his box and talked to
him while I carefully sketched his little round form in
the notebook I used for my poetry. We looked into each
other's eyes. What sort of bird was he? I still don't know.
What matters is that in the silence of my tiny bedroom
he spoke to me of survival and hope. I had no idea how
lonely I was in that place, until he came to keep me company. So when I awoke very early one morning to find
him lying on the floor of his cardboard prison, I sobbed.

At nineteen, I did not understand the inevitability of death. There was no choice but to consign him to a small hole scraped out with a spoon beneath one of the straggly rose bushes in the cottage garden, then dash miserably to set the refectory tables for breakfast.

When, at the end of 1980, my first husband and I moved out of London to the countryside just outside Bath, I was reduced to screaming hysteria at the sight of a mouse on the bedside table, nibbling chocolates from my Christmas stocking. The creature was a terrifying affront; it broached my citadel. But about ten years later my son Dan became custodian of a white rat used in biology lessons for observation. He named this rat Ozric (after a Somerset space rock band he liked, called Ozric Tentacles) and formed a close relationship with the intelligent creature who would run across our wide garden when called, shimmy up Dan's body as if up a cliff face, and sit on his shoulder, preening fine whiskers. Ozric lived both at school and with us in a large glass tank, and I loved to walk around with him curled around my neck, pink nose and inquisitive eyes on one side, long pink tail and enormous testicles on the other.

Yes, we can change.

And the change is exhilarating.

Looking back, I realise that during all the pet-free years (despite the subtle encroachments I describe) my latent unhappiness was caused by a wilful clinging to complexity. When I started to write novels my preoccupation was with hidden symbolism and melancholy *meaning* rather than good, crisp, clear story. It was all so angst-ridden. Politics, relationships, religion, ambition, envy of others' success, anxiety and rage about the environment… Everything bothered me and I had no answers. The lessons provided by Mole and Ratty, by Tarka the Otter, by Micky, by Fred, by Ozric all went unheard. There was little to alleviate the sometimes terrible stress of family life (caused principally by my daughter's congenital illness) and my restless need to write, to broadcast, to 'keep up' with a successful husband at the same time as being the kind of mother children want to be with. Not to mention the perfect wife and hostess. Sometimes all of it drove me down into a dark lair I could not disclose to a soul.

But with the advent of a cat called Dizzy, then Billie the Labrador, things started to shift, although I did not know it. The pets provided family therapy for all of us, but especially me. There had been no simplicity before; now it was forced by the essential needs of a dog and a cat (and, later, dogs and cats) which knew no other joy than to be fed, to be stroked and to snooze in a warm place. These animals force the human ego to halt its neurotic preoccupations and realise that after birth and before death there is this shining thing called Life. It is paw prints through wet grass in a summer dawn. It is a wordless grunt of contentment when an ear is scratched. It is the dancing thrill of a feather or leaf that must be chased. When at last you comprehend the ease with which the essence of life is expressed in a purr and a wag, you are diverted to a new path through the woods. It is the one I still walk, frequently astonished by my own ignorance and by the generosity of a world of trees, grass, flowers and animals that constantly feeds the soul and is ready to forgive.

Forgive? Ah, anthropomorphism: the attribution of human thoughts and emotions to non-human things. The worst of sins. The unacceptable face of squishy, squelchy sentimentality. As adults we are not supposed to believe that the mice in the root systems of Brambly Hedge enjoy small mirror images of our own lives, with hopes and dreams and naughty babies in high chairs too. Of course not. We must realise that Peter Rabbit has myxomatosis and will die a terrible, blind death, that Tarka will savage the ducklings while Christopher Robin's wise old 'Wol' will have no mercy on vole or mouse. This is how nature is – and we might as well tell our children so. While we are at it, point out to them that their pets do not 'love' or 'feel jealous' or 'sad' – because they are not human. The mother duck will not grieve for her lost ducklings, nor will the mother dog for her puppy-farmed litter … so don't worry about her, darling.

But when on the last evening of the nineteenth century, Thomas Hardy heard a storm-blasted and bedraggled thrush singing its heart out on a branch, the great man suspected the 'frail, gaunt and small' bird knew something he did not. Since there was no reason to sound so damned cheerful, the little creature's 'ecstatic sound' must indicate 'some blessed Hope' of which the pessimistic human being knew nothing. But birds do not 'hope'. Nor are they 'happy' although their song may sound carefree.

They sing to mark out territory and attract mates, not to express any mood with human significance. No matter. The purpose of that bird was to bring a message to the listener and change his mood. It was a divine messenger, and the morose poet merely the blessed recipient of an accidental wisdom greater than himself.

And that is how I feel about all my own animal guides.

The growth of empathy is surely the single most vital ingredient for our survival as a species. When we think of animals in human terms we reach out with heart and soul, projecting our imagination into their world and becoming better and wiser as a result. It is the best sort of exercise for a child who loves a special toy and worries about its feelings. The idea is expressed to perfection in one of the most sublime children's books ever written, *The Velveteen Rabbit* by Margery Williams, first published in 1922 and in print ever since. The sub-title is 'How Toys Become Real' – and the point is, they are made 'real' by being believed in and loved. As the old Skin Horse explains to the little rabbit: 'Real isn't how you are made ... It's a thing that happens to you. When a child loves you for a long, long time, not just to play with, but REALLY loves you, then you become Real.'

When the rabbit asks if this process hurts, the honest horse replies: 'Sometimes ... When you are Real you don't mind being hurt.'

This process is what Williams calls 'nursery magic' – and we would do well to listen to it, and to the music of Pan in *The Wind in the Willows*. We would be transformed if only we could hear. Making the imaginative leap into the 'mind' of a toy can be (should be) the first step towards projecting yourself into the experience of an animal – and the true miracle in this transaction is that as a result it is *you* who becomes more 'real'. The child who believes his precious objects have feelings (oh, the genius of the *Toy Story* series...) could never grow to be an adult who is cruel to animals. The adult who believes that animals, birds, trees and the soil itself all have lessons to teach will never under-value that powerful reality, nor stand by and watch others destroy it. The human being who attributes to every living thing such a value that he or she can hear those organisms utter their own profound truths ... that person is humble enough to allow the smallest, briefest butterfly its vital glory within the whole. Let each ordinary cabbage white speak – and be sure to listen, with reverence and love.

Believe me, I could write none of this, were it not for my dog.

In January 2015 I was working at my desk at home when my husband called me outside. He looked anxious. Bonnie followed me outside and into the field across from our front door, the one that leads past the ruin of the old mill and leat to the abandoned dam and millpond. I could hear the sound immediately – a terrified high-pitched keening.

'Look,' he said.

On the other side of the river I spotted movement. A small brown creature was running hither and thither in the dank undergrowth, disappearing then reappearing, and crying all the while. It was a baby otter, calling pitifully. Bonnie stared across, worried by those relentless, panicky squeaks. (In Zoroastrian belief the otter is revered as a 'water dog', so perhaps she recognised the language of that little lost soul). We watched for long minutes, wondering what to do, while the pup continued its frightened 'hunting around in a circle with pleading whine' – just like little Portly. It must have become separated from its mother; would she come back? Not if we were standing there. Suppose she had been run over on the lane? Can you rescue a wild creature? Should Robin don waders and try to catch it? If he succeeded, and the mother did return, that would be a disaster. I rushed inside to consult the internet and even messaged the wildlife cameraman and photographer Charlie Hamilton-James, who used to be our neighbour on the river and is an otter expert. All the time, as Robin watched, the crying continued and the baby ran about in acute distress.

The consensus was to leave the pup, in the hope that the mother would hear it and return. But Charlie Hamilton-James messaged me (the wonder of it is that he was in Montana at the time) that an otter mother might abandon a pup if it seems weak ... and that was a blunt reminder of the limits of happy anthropomorphism. Poor little Portly may not be wanted any more, no anxious otter daddy waiting by the weir. Feeling helpless, I returned to the safety of my desk, but Robin was vigilant, going out again and again to see where the baby was, until at last there was no sight or sound of the little creature. We rejoiced in the belief that Mum had come back and the otters were reunited in the holt. Neither of us voiced the thought that a fox might have taken the pup.

The next morning (rather later than usual) Robin pulled open the curtains and cried, 'Oh no!' There on the grass below our bedroom window was the baby otter, lying still. We threw on bathrobes and rushed downstairs and out into the grey, cold morning. My husband knelt to scoop up the pup. He thought he felt warmth. He *did* feel warmth. Maybe it was still alive. So we carried the little otter into the kitchen and I spread out a towel on the worktop and instinctively massaged its chest. And a dropper with warm milk at the corner of the mouth … these are the things you do, not knowing what else there is to do, because something must be done. I massaged and stroked and whispered *Come on, little one, come on…* But of course it was dead.

What upset us most was the fact that the animal had struggled so far from the river to the house. He had some-how managed to climb two banks to find his way into the garden and covered about 40 metres. Here I notice how, having carefully called the pup 'it', I have started, without thinking, to use 'he'. Male or female … it doesn't matter. The slippage occurs because I couldn't help but think of the animal as needy, like a human, and imagine he had made a deliberate journey to the house to get help. You can't avoid such a projection, no more than Robin could help cursing the fact that he had not woken earlier, when the animal might have been alive, when we might have saved him. Of course I don't really believe that the otter pup decided to walk from his own element towards ours because he felt instinctively that the humans might help him. Of course not. Still, he was beneath our window, and that was so unlikely it felt like a message.

Nothing could be done. Never again would I be so close to such an elusive child of the wild. Feeling a mixture of joy and awe at the sad privilege, I held one of the pup's broad brown paws, kissed the beautiful flat head with greyer fur around the face, lifted the muscular tail and caressed the magnificent, velvety coat. How beautiful it was. Such a small creature, lying dead in our kitchen – yet such a large event for us. We decided we must bury (with due ceremony) the pup on the bank by the river which would have been its home – but it wasn't to be. Charlie Hamilton-James messaged me about the

Otter Project at Cardiff University, a long-term envi-
ronmental surveillance scheme using otters found dead
by members of the public in order to investigate con-
taminants, disease and population biology. It was our
duty to give up the pup to science. So the next day a
pleasant man arrived with a bin-bag and took it away,
leaving us with a lasting memory of one baby otter, and
another lesson in mortality and tenderness from the
animal kingdom.

CHAPTER SIX

And then they heard the angels tell
'Who were the first to cry Nowell?
Animals all, as it befell,
In the stable where they did dwell!
Joy shall be theirs in the morning!'

<small>From the Field Mice's Carol in *The Wind in the Willows*</small>
<small>by Kenneth Grahame (1859–1932)</small>

C HRISTMAS WAS APPROACHING. We managed
to solve the problem of our annual card – which
always featured a 'storytelling' photograph of

our little dog, with an uplifting and unexpected message inside. This year's would incorporate all the images of Bonnie from ten years, ending with the last one inside, and its prescient caption, 'Believe in angels...' – followed by her dates. It seemed important to us that people knew that she was dead – and I offer this as an important message for people who love their animals. There is nothing to be ashamed of in mourning; nothing to apologise for in wishing others to know that you are sad to lose your friend.

This year writing the cards became more than a merry Christmas greeting to friends, family and colleagues. It was an act of remembrance.

Everywhere I went, I thought about my dog. She trotted beside me unseen when I was out and about, and sat beside my desk while I was working. I felt her in the room, I heard her in the wind, the rain pattered tiny paw-steps, and I even scented her from time to time, my own nose quivering like a hound's. That small presence was like a flickering light, a will o' the wisp in my imagination, leading me onwards.

With Bonnie at my side or leading ahead, I stumbled numbly on – although I could not have predicted how many surprises were in store. For example, four weeks after buying the sorrowful Sarah Gillespie mezzotint called *Absence*, another work of art called to me from a gallery wall. This one had an animal voice.

Art has been my passion since, as a twelve-year-old, I would be allowed to leave our council flat in Liverpool, walk down to the bus stop, alight in William Brown Street and spend hours at the Walker Art Gallery. In the school holidays I might do this once a fortnight in an era (the late '50s) which now seems so much more innocent and safe. My character was shaped equally by our local library in Old Swan and by the Walker. Everything about the place made my spirits soar: the pillared portico, the marble statues of Michelangelo and Raphael at the entrance, the high crowded galleries in rich jewel colours. I sought out the same pictures again and again, and stood entranced before them. The sensuous beauty of the Pre-Raphaelites fascinated this plain, bespectacled child who fell in love with red-haired women who looked as if they might bend languorously from the frames to rescue me. My favourite picture in the whole collection was *Virgin and Child in Glory*, by Murillo. I was lonely; in the calm, compassionate gaze of the Virgin and baby Jesus, and the froth of lovely putti all around them, I found acceptance and peace.

On a bright Saturday at the end of November 2015 we walked into Larkhall Fine Art in Bath and there, in a mixed show of prints, I saw the Eric Gill woodcut. This 1916 work illustrates the lines from *The Wind in the Willows* which appear at the top of this chapter, the second and third ones cut around three sides of the image. In the book, the incident happens in the tender chapter called 'Dulce Domum'. Mole and Rat are hurrying through a village in the snow, glimpsing other lives through uncurtained windows, when suddenly Mole catches the scent of his own 'sweet home', abandoned at the beginning of the story when he encountered swashbuckling Ratty on the river bank. This particular section of a book written for children is one of the most profoundly beautiful invocations of Home in the whole of literature. Mole is ashamed of his bleak, dusty little burrow, abandoned without thought. But Rat, a true friend, transforms the unexpected, poignant homecoming into 'great joy and contentment'.

Mole and Rat are just about to begin a rather meagre supper when the field mice arrive to sing Christmas carols outside Mole End. All of this came back to me as I looked at the Eric Gill woodcut. What thrilled me in that moment was the message honouring animals. The Christmas image in silhouette is beautiful: the Virgin and Child are seated in the stable on the left and baby Jesus reaches out excitedly with both arms towards the group of patient creatures who have come to worship. A bird flies down from the sky, two slender long-horned oxen stare at the baby, while at their feet are seated a sheep, a squirrel and, on the right, a strange little animal which can only be a dog. You would suppose the creature a fox, with pointed muzzle and pricked-up ears, but the tail is all wrong, not bushy but thin. How odd of Gill to place a dog at the Nativity.

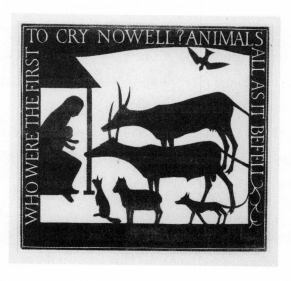

There is an intensely pure stillness in the animals' gaze as they are blessed by the Holy Child. The image moved me deeply, and it was with my lost dog in mind that I bought the woodcut. This time the act of remembrance (for that is what it was) did not feel like a haunting but a hymn of celebration. I love the idea that the animals were the first to recognise the holiness of the Nativity, that they were blessed. No, that they *are* blessed. Why shouldn't they be?

A companion animal becomes an essential part of the idea of home. The process amounts to more than the purring or excited yelping which says *Welcome*, or the comfort gained from the sight of a familiar basket in the corner. It is far more the thought Kenneth Grahame bestows on his affectionate Mole – an almost sacred recognition of 'the special value of some such anchorage in one's existence'. At the stage when I was deracinated by the loss of a marriage and a home, my little dog became the anchor. When I was lost she found me. Wherever we were together was home. This was the consolation I expressed in *A Small Dog Saved My Life*:

> *The one thing you can be sure of is that your dog will recognise you, no matter what mask you wear.*

Your dog will know your voice, even when all you can utter is a cry.

Your dog will love you no matter what you have become.

No matter where you are, your dog will welcome you home.

🐕 🐕 🐕 🐕

Our home contained no dog. Within those familiar, beloved walls, surrounded by the clutter of pictures, books, cushions and *objets* that is my style, and blessed by family ... I was nevertheless *homesick* for my dog. My love for Bonnie was now 'un-homed': still making me unhappy, I knew it would nevertheless slowly move into memory, and that thought made me even more bereft.

A friend wrote telling me how sad she was at the death of her very old cat: 'Now, when I come into the house, I miss that sense that this is a home where an animal lives.' That was exactly how we felt – and in those early weeks it made me desperate. It was a sort of madness that took us to visit a litter of Havanese puppies in a village near Bath. My husband was unwilling, but I insisted. The breeders were delightful, the pedigrees impeccable, the puppies adorable – if very expensive. I imagined what it would be like to start again with a puppy, training from scratch a baby dog with no 'emotional' history, no unknown damage. But of course it was wrong to go to see the puppies in a mood of panic and loss. I was behaving like somebody stunned after a fall from a horse, blundering about a field trying to find another one to saddle.

When we arrived back home that day my husband told me decisively that we would certainly give a home to another little dog one day – but we would only think of a rescue dog. I knew he was right. There are many beautiful puppies bred by responsible, expert breeders, and maybe it would be fun to choose one – but Bonnie had been left tied to a tree, and animal rescue shelters, large and small, are full of unwanted animals who could be made happy in a 'forever home'. This, he said, would be the right thing to do.

When a beloved pet dies some people are so overwhelmed by grief they cry, 'Never again.' I once knew a man and a woman, passionate dog lovers both, whose marriage was (in truth) helped by their dog, Peppy. When the old dog died they immediately cleared away all signs of her life and settled, each of them, unspeaking, into a lonely, permanent grief. In vain did I suggest (months later) a visit to the Cats' and Dogs' Home, even showing them a feature in the local newspaper with a row of beseeching canine faces, needing homes. 'No, we could never go through that again,' the couple said – and that was final. The mourning must be permanent and their cottage, garden and surrounding fields (perfect space) continue to be dog-free. Theirs was the anguish expressed by Rudyard Kipling in his bleak poem 'The Power of the Dog':

> *There is sorrow enough in the natural way*
> *From men and women to fill our day;*
> *But when we are certain of sorrow in store,*
> *Why do we always arrange for more?*
> *Brothers and sisters, I bid you beware*
> *Of giving your heart to a dog to tear.*

Kipling warns that a puppy brings 'love unflinching that cannot lie' but that for a human being to love the animal is 'to risk your heart'. Why? Because after 'the fourteen years which Nature permits'…

When the body that lived at your single will,
When the whimper of welcome is stilled (how still!),
When the spirit that answered your every mood
Is gone – wherever it goes – for good,
You still discover how much you care
And will give your heart to a dog to tear!

When Bonnie died I read this poem (and many others, since poetry is where I find rest) again and again, but my instinctive response to that terror of being hurt was to shout, 'I will not be afraid, but let my heart be ready to be torn again, whenever that shall be.' And naturally I thought deeply about Kipling's phrase 'wherever it goes'. Where does the spirit go? I had asked that question on Remembrance Sunday, and when I felt Bonnie move behind me on the bed.

Little did I know that very soon events would make me ask it again, in even greater wonderment.

The Christmas cards were sent. My week of illness came to an end and very early in the morning on

Friday 18 December, six weeks after Bonnie's death, I woke from one of the most vivid dreams I have ever experienced. Sometimes you do not 'have' a dream, but experience a whole new way of being (even if only for seconds) which can be life-changing. So it was this time. In the dream Bonnie appeared and talked to me. She was not ill and old as I last saw her, but bright and assertive – and oddly large. As I recall it, her head was as big as mine … how strange. Quite clearly I heard my dog speak. She instructed me to write a cheque to an animal shelter south of Shepton Mallet in Somerset, called Happy Landings. Without hesitation I promised her that I would.

This was the fourth sign.

Around 2012 I had been approached by a friend and neighbour and asked to lend my name to this small animal charity, as a patron. Nothing would be required of me; 'names' can be useful for future fundraising, that's all. I said yes, of course – and made the forty-minute drive to visit the place. There I met dedicated volunteers, led by Lyn Southway, inspected premises in urgent need of repair, heard terrible stories of dogs thrown from moving cars, newborn puppies and kittens abandoned in freezing conditions, dogs brutalised by chain whips then dumped, and so on. I learned how long it takes for a battery hen to recover its feathers after incarceration, and realised that no gerbil, rabbit, donkey or goat in need would be turned away from Happy Landings. Convinced by the good work, I told them to get in touch if they needed help with any fundraising initiative. There was talk of an event that I would co-host … but in the end nothing happened. Nevertheless, I mentioned the charity in my *Daily Mail* column and kind readers sent donations, so some good was achieved.

I admit I had not thought about Happy Landings for a very long time, nor been in touch for about four years. For most of us, there are too many calls on time, concern and money … and in any case, since my last contact I had become a grandmother three times over, and watched my parents grow more frail as they entered their nineties. There was no residual guilt in this inactive 'patron'.

So where did that vivid dream come from? I awoke in a state of great agitation knowing it would be impossible to get back to sleep unless I obeyed my dog's orders. It was just before 4 a.m. Bizarrely, I was convinced that it would not do to wait until morning; action had to be taken there and then. Therefore I got out of bed, put on slippers and dressing gown, and crept downstairs to my freezing study. First I took one of our last remaining Christmas cards and wrote it to Lyn Southway (I even had to look up her name because I could not remember) and to the animals at Happy Landings. Then I wrote a proper letter, apologising for my long silence and explaining that, as our little dog had recently died and I was utterly bereft, I wanted to make a donation to help feed the animals in the sanctuary over the Christmas season. Finally I scribbled a generous cheque and shoved it in the card. All this took a very short time, but I could not return to bed until the envelope was sealed and addressed and stamped.

My final act was the strangest of all. In 2010 I'd set up a Facebook page ('Bonnie the Maltese Dog') in my dog's name to help market my books. At her death it became another focus for much shared sympathy. Now, in the cold, black morning, I quickly called it up and bashed out these words:

This is Bonnie's spirit writing with ethereal paws. I woke Bel from sleep to make her realise she had to make a Christmas donation to Happy Landings Animal Shelter in

*Somerset. They do wonderful work and that's why she is a
patron. So I'm watching her at her desk now, at just after
4.30 a.m., writing a cheque in a card to the team (led
by Lyn) and the assorted creatures they care for so well.*

You could see it as a flourish of the imagination to write
a post in the persona of my dog, but that's how the Facebook page worked – and it is always good to give publicity
to any charity. On the other hand you could regard this as
yet more evidence that the bereft dog-lover was becoming more and more batty. No matter, I returned to bed
feeling calmer and happier than I had in weeks, and slept
deeply. Something good had happened. In the morning
I described the events of the night to my husband and
he smiled enigmatically as he held out his hand to take
the envelope to post. It was easy for him to accept that
Bonnie would inevitably visit me in a dream.

The following week I received a grateful email from
the charity to let me know the cheque had arrived,
despite Christmas postal delays, and I thought no more
about it. Christmas was upon us. The house was decorated and there was food to buy. My best friend and her
husband were arriving with their dog, Bertie. Presents

were piled under the tree, labelled with love for four generations and our friends.

This Christmas we would all be blessed by the presence of a new baby, but diminished by Bonnie's absence. That would not do. So I took the shallow cardboard box containing her ashes and placed it on top of the row of wide bookshelves at the far end of the sitting room, where I always place our simple pottery Nativity scene, made by the sculptor Emma Maiden. I covered the box with a white napkin, and then placed Mary and Joseph, the angel and baby in his crib on top of it, as if on a snowy dais, with shepherds, magi and animals ranged just below. It was perfect. When, on Christmas morning, I quietly revealed to my parents that Bonnie was still there 'with' us all, my mother (not normally given to sentimentality, unlike her husband and daughter) could not restrain her tears.

All my father could say was, 'Quite right too.'

＊ ＊ ＊ ＊

On the morning of New Year's Eve I lay in bed with a cup of tea. Hanging on the wall over the fireplace opposite our bed is a large framed portrait (taken in August 2009 by Bath photographer Neill Menneer) of the small 'pack' which, until so recently, inhabited this old house. Robin stands on the left, I am on the right, clutching Bonnie in my arms. She looks almost intolerably pretty, with her back legs hanging down, fur so white and well-groomed, and a flash of pink stomach revealed. We all look very happy; in fact, the dog looks positively smug. Missing her, I gazed at the image, and reflected that 2016 – the first year without her – would soon begin. I was wondering how long this would go on ... the underlying sadness that must be concealed amid the happy bustle of family life, especially in the season of peace, goodwill and festivity.

Then something truly bizarre happened. It is very hard to describe – because essentially absurd and unbelievable. Disbelief is natural, and cynicism is an essential part of the *zeitgeist*. Yet the strange truth of these unexpected events must be told because they revealed to me that Bonnie's death was just the beginning of a quest. And here was another signpost.

Maybe I knew that. In any case, seconds later, I seized the notebook by my bed and scrawled:

I was staring at our triple portrait over the mantelpiece in the bedroom, focussing on Bonnie in my arms, when suddenly she seemed to shimmer. It appeared almost that she was moving, almost as if trying to wriggle out of the arms of the woman in the photo who held her tightly — and leap towards the same woman (tired and melancholy) who lay in bed looking at her. I blinked hard then took off my glasses, inspected them, wiped them on the edge of the duvet, then put them back. Still she shimmered, like a mirage in the desert.

Looking back now, as I read those words, I visualise a scene in book or film, as when (for example) the ship in the picture on the wall comes to life in *The Voyage of the Dawn Treader*. One moment the image is flat, unreal, one-dimensional; next, the wind fills the sails, the waves toss, and the distant cry of seabirds can be heard. Reality shivers along the wafer-thin interface between two worlds; rationality slides down the hillside, helpless in a slippage of scree.

Just for those few seconds, my shining little dog seemed animated, as if she wanted me to know something.

Ah, but there I write with hindsight.

At the time, of course, I cherished no fantasy that this was a message; I just knew the experience was not imaginary. It was not a trick of the light or eyesight, nor was I on medication or suffering from a hangover. No wishful thinking makes me look at a photograph and will it to become something it is not. The picture was ahead in my eye line; I gazed – and for a brief moment there was a transformation. This was so vivid that as well as writing it down, I had to tell my down-to-earth, practical husband. Acutely missing Bonnie, as he does, he simply stared at me. What comment can be made when your wife is telling you about a vision – which she will later count as the fifth sign?

(Every single day since then have I looked at that picture, with chronically short-sighted, unaided eyes and with spectacles and with the perfect vision of contact lenses. Of course, it has never since shimmered or glowed or appeared in any way to move or shine. It is a photograph in a frame on a bedroom wall. That's all. Yet I confess that sometimes, when I glance at it through a myopic haze I can imagine that my hands crossed to hold up my dog are like the second wings of cherubim, folded across in front.)

Just over two hours after the weird mirage incident, an email from the Happy Landings Animal Shelter appeared in my inbox. It said:

Hi Bel

I'm sure it's way too soon to be talking about another dog when I know how much of a hole Bonnie has left and how utterly heartbreaking that is.

I also know that you would be honest and happily say that this is the case, but it's one of those agonising

*decisions on my part as to whether to ask or not – and it
has taken me days to email you! I didn't want there to be
the opportunity of this possible little dog for adoption and
not ask – only for you to say in a few weeks' time that you
wished I had! So please forgive me if timing is rubbish but
this is meant with good intentions.*

Kind regards
Lyn

There was no photograph attached, which struck me
as admirably sensitive. I thought about replying for two
hours, before emailing to say that I did not mind the suggestion at all – and what *is* this little dog? The reply did
not come back until four hours had passed:

Bel, I didn't want to add photo just in case!!

*She is called Sophia and a most loving little girl. Would,
I'm sure, be just a little nervous to start. She is two years
old and a Yorkie x Chihuahua.*

With this was an attachment that proved impossible

to open. What was to be done? I did not want another dog, not yet, not eight weeks after Bonnie's death, yet I was drawn to this message and desperately wanted to see this dog. So I emailed yet again to request the pictures in another form, and one hour later, at last, I saw two images on my screen. What a strange little animal. It looks like a fox cub, reddish-tan, with pointed muzzle and pricked-up ears, but the tail is all wrong, not bushy but thin…

I could hear a clatter from my kitchen, where my son was cooking dinner for New Year's Eve. The pictures were on my screen – bright and mesmerising. I called Robin, showed him and announced that I had fallen in love.

Soon champagne was opened to begin the evening that leads to the turn of the year.

For over ten years I have been writing an advice column, first in *The Times* and then in the *Daily Mail*. Week after week I study sad letters from people whose lives are in a mess, often because they do not talk their problems through with those who should be closest to them, often because they lurch from one emotional upheaval to another, making no plans and rarely stopping to unpick the problem in order to find a way through. They become stuck within stress, blinded by tears. My counsel is generally along the lines of … you know … take deep breaths, be calm, ponder options, think and talk things through point by point. And so on.

Yet here I was, possibly hurtling towards a new pet, with no careful thought, no real conversation, no plan. *Quis custodiet ipsos custodes?* asks the old Latin tag. Who guards the guards themselves? Who counsels the counsellor?

On 2 January we drove to Happy Landings to see the little dog. Lyn Southway explained that she was handed in because of a family break-up. It seems that the couple concerned had four children and another dog; that their life was chaos, with an intolerable level of dysfunction and even a possible suggestion of domestic violence. Whatever the facts, they had decided to split just before Christmas and had to get rid of the two dogs. Usually attempts will be made to rehome a pair of dogs together, but these two small ones were being fostered until separate homes could be found, since Lyn and experienced foster-carers Brian and Julie judged that they would thrive better apart.

So there she was, looking so anxious in Brian's arms, nestled inside his jacket because it was so cold: a tiny fox-like creature called Sophia, with neat paws and bright, jet-button eyes. She had a Chihuahua head, domed with widely spaced bat-ears, honey-coloured fronds that stuck out each side of her face, but a rough, dark, brindled body. Her tan legs were neat and smooth; her black-and-tan tail pointed. What an odd little mixture this dog was: a waif-and-stray mutt. Exquisite Bonnie was pure Maltese – white and silky with a whisk of a tail that curled over her back. They could not be more different, except in one respect: tightly curled up in a ball to sleep, each could fit on a dinner plate.

I held out my arms to take her and, even though she was shivering with fear, not cold, she licked my face. Brian explained that when he first collected her she was transfixed with terror and 'just cried'.

What could I do to control this powerful compulsion to take care of her? To make up for all the bad things that might have happened to her in a household where she was not really nurtured? This little dog was crying out to be loved in a peaceful home.

But it is too soon.

Isn't it?

Need to consider, need to talk.

Need to think.

Need to reflect on the spirit of the lost dog, who still inhabits our house. Is it a betrayal of love, to give a home to another animal? Will an impulse rooted in grief be strong enough to cope with any problems?

After a short while we left and drove home. Brian's last words were in my ears: 'Oh, I think you're going to see her again.' Of course, the man was right. He must have seen the dog-shaped hole in our eyes and hearts, as well as how we behaved with this little orphan. After all, doggy people just *know*.

A few days later Lyn Southway brought the little dog to us, so she could meet Dan's Labrador, Dotty, since we have to spend time with her. But Sophia growled and yapped and trembled, and nobody could describe the visit as a resounding success. Nevertheless, just over a week later we drove back to the animal shelter to collect the little mutt and take her home. She was to be called Sophie (rather than the more formal Sophia), which means 'wisdom'. This felt so right. For even at the time I was aware of a vein of uncanny wisdom running through these events – not in the sense of rational knowledge, but of a much deeper, stranger understanding that defies rational explanation. Not learning – but enlightenment.

Just consider the sequence:

1. If I had not dreamed that Bonnie gave me clear instructions, I would not have written to Happy Landings.
2. If I had not written, Lyn Southway would not have known my little dog had died.
3. If Lyn had not known, she would not (obviously) have contacted me about Sophie – and on the very day that the image of Bonnie in the portrait in our bedroom seemed to come alive before my eyes.

And there is one more thing. Hearing about Sophie, meeting her and deciding to adopt her was all very sudden, but a few weeks later I was able to clarify the timeline.

4. The date Sophie was handed into Happy Landings was the very same date as my original dream.

So how could I be in any doubt that the blessing of one little dog had led me to another – a fox-like creature who stepped down from an Eric Gill Nativity, and into our life?

CHAPTER SEVEN

There is a water over which the soul of one who has died must
pass. And there is a dog there, a little black dog with a white
spot on its throat. And one must ask permission from that dog
to pass, so that one may travel on, to reach that other level,
where those who have died are waiting...

RAMON MEDINA SILVA, HUICHOL SHAMAN (D. 1971)

P EOPLE SAY YOU do not always choose a pet; sometimes a pet chooses you. The other day, in a plant
nursery, one of the employees, a woman in late
middle age, told me at length how she had vowed not to

get another cat when her old cat died. 'I was so unhappy I decided I just couldn't go through it again, and anyway, I'm *so* busy…' Then one day, a stray arrived in her back garden: filthy, matted, with weeping eyes and infested with fleas. She left food out for the animal, placing it closer, closer… and weeks later he was eating by the back door. Still later he had moved into the house. He even allowed her to bath him, revealing a beautiful ginger-and-white puss, like a transformation in a fairy tale. Now her life is made joyful by the presence of the cat who follows her everywhere, even into the bathroom.

'I said to him this morning, "A lady needs to go to the loo in private!"' She beamed so happily as she told me her story, and Sophie ran around our feet. 'Sometimes it just feels *right*,' she said and I nodded.

A strange quirk of fate had led the little dog to our home, only ten weeks after Bonnie died, but this never felt like a 'replacement'. How could it, when Bonnie was unique – as every single much-loved pet is unique? Nor did it feel disloyal, as I knew that the new dog, so different, would elicit a fresh set of feelings. For one thing, she would sleep in the kitchen, not on our bed. What's more, she would be *our* pet, whereas Bonnie was really 'mine'.

Sophie felt strange too: a rough little wild-looking crea-ture, spiky in coat and in manner, not a lapdog like my precious, soft Maltese. I thought of her as a changeling – left by the fairies in Bonnie's basket, in the manner of all those folk tales I devoured as a child.

She had, of course, a job to fulfil. Bonnie followed me everywhere and I depended on her company during the day when writing. Naturally Sophie could not realise this was her role, but it did not take long before she followed me to the desk, then stood, looking puzzled, wonder-ing what to do. She had only known a hectic, unhappy home, full of screams – the natural noise of four young children and the terrible sound of warring adults. Now she stalked suspiciously around her new, peaceful home with an air of amazement.

When she had been with us about ten days, something strange happened. Bonnie's handsome wicker bed, lined with a red cushion, used to have a permanent place against the wall to the left of my desk. (The-dog-with-many-beds also had that fateful soft blue and red-rose patterned bed in which she died, another berth up in Robin's attic office, and a round basket with a handle from Kenya that stood in a particular corner of the kitchen/breakfast room).

When she died we moved that same wicker bed, the lining freshly laundered, into store (and cleared all the others away too), but when Sophie arrived, like a premature baby, we placed it in the breakfast room near the stove. There was nothing in my study where it had been. Instead, I'd put a cushion on the opposite side of my desk, ready for when she understood her role as writing companion within this household.

On this particular day Sophie wandered around my desk, still exploring, then stopped stock still, staring intently at a spot on the carpet by the wall – where the wicker bed used to be. Her shoulders were hunched, tail down, bat-ears pricked forward, nose pointing at the vacancy where once Bonnie slept. The tension in her body was palpable. Her pose reminded me of the savage dog in a famous Francis Bacon picture – frozen, threatened and bleak. Something inexplicable was worrying this new little dog; it rooted her to that spot for eight minutes (I watched the time passing on my computer as I stayed silent), until I took pity and bent to scoop her up, telling her that everything was all right, that we were all going to be happy together.

I don't see how Sophie could have possibly picked up

Bonnie's scent, because the basket was no longer there and if the carpet it once stood on (raised on legs) smelt of anything it would have been dust. So what had transfixed her? Many people would interpret her anxious stillness, her staring at one spot, as evidence that she had seen, or at least sensed, something invisible. That somehow she had picked up the aura of the dead animal, hovering around that specific place in the room which was now completely empty. I realise how implausible this will sound to the sceptic. Nevertheless, I report what I saw: a very small dog concentrating every iota of anxious, questing energy at a vacant spot where another dog had not been for many weeks.

Not long afterwards came another odd incident. As she grew older I used to carry Bonnie in a grey, padded pet shoulder bag, with a zipped top for security and space at one end for her head to look out. We had to take Sophie in the car and I decided to try her in it, even though it had never been washed, so would be laden with Bonnie's scent. But that had no effect, because Sophie loved the carrier, so much so that on some occasions she refused to get out, clearly feeling very secure. One night, instead of hanging it up on the hook by the back door, I left the bag (unzipped, of course) right next to her basket on the floor in the breakfast room and she chose it, jumping in to curl happily inside.

But when I came down the following morning there was an empty space where bag and dog had been. For a split second I did a double take, then saw with surprise that the bag – with Sophie still curled at the bottom – was now standing exactly where Bonnie's round Kenyan basket used to be. That corner was two full strides from where we'd left Sophie the night before – and what's more, with an armchair in the way. Robin suggested that Sophie might have jumped out of the bag, making it roll over, and then jumped back, making it move some more.

But to have done this so many times during the night that the bag moved two metres, including a necessary right angle to skirt an armchair? And after this random rolling and moving activity, to have landed, right way up, exactly where Bonnie's basket used to sit?

It was unfeasible and bizarre, but Robin could come up with no other explanation. Supposing instead the little dog had decided (as if!) to move the bag by jumping out and dragging it by the handles with her tiny teeth, why did she choose (as if!) to drag it to that very spot, before jumping back in and going back to sleep? No, that was entirely unbelievable too. So was there a poltergeist in our house that night, a supernatural creature who decided to teach me a lesson by moving this dog to the previous dog's favourite spot? Or was this an example of the paranormal, telekinesis – where a strange mental force can move objects, and therefore the pervasive spirit of Bonnie was exerting power to move the pet carrier, Sophie and all?

Of course not! Nobody sensible believes in ghosts, do they? I suppose Robin's explanation had to be correct – and yet the episode remained a mystery. Thinking of one other remote possibility, I assure you neither of us has ever sleep-walked. So deep in my heart, unspoken, I could not help surmising that Bonnie's death, still so fresh, was influencing events, in a way that had no rational explanation.

Animals have more highly developed instincts than humans and can sense weather changes and coming natural phenomena, like a tsunami or an earthquake. How do they do that? How could I be sure that my new little dog was not sensing the energy of the old dog, and sending messages? Despite seeking rational explanations, I could not be sure.

What do dogs know about death? I had witnessed Dotty's curious agitation, when she sensed (rather than saw) the still-frozen corpse of Bonnie lying on the table and then came, quite deliberately, to offer me comfort. Naturally I knew all the stories about the grief of dogs, and had also seen videos online about how dogs pine for their own kind too, and for companion animals of different species they have been housed with. Now Sophie's behaviour made me wonder afresh what exactly dogs know, what abilities they have that we can only dream of.

In the spring of 2014 we witnessed a strange incident involving Bonnie. On holiday in Cornwall we went to

Daymer Bay and took the pleasant walk across the golf course by the sea to visit the tiny church of St Enodoc, founded 700 years ago. Wind-driven sand has formed banks that are almost level with the roof on two sides; the odd little spire pokes up like a slightly bent finger saying, 'Come.' From the sixteenth century to the middle of the nineteenth century, the church was virtually buried by the dunes, but in order to maintain the tithes required by the Church of England, it had to host services at least once a year. So the vicar and parishioners had to climb in through a hole in the roof. By 1864 it was unearthed and the dunes were stabilised. For me this was a place of pilgrimage since the poet John Betjeman spent many childhood holidays in Trebetherick, immortalised St Enodoc in one of his best-loved poems, and is buried in the churchyard there.

When Robin and I approached the lych gate, we were very pleased to note that the old 'lych stone' was still there. Visiting churches and churchyards is one of our interests. The lych gate was where the pall-bearers would stop, often resting on built-in benches each side after setting the coffin down on the lych stone, a long, low, narrow stone 'table'. The vicar or priest would walk to the lych gate to meet the corpse (Anglo-Saxon *lic*) and then conduct it on to holy ground, on the next stage of its journey, walking ahead of the cortège and intoning, 'I am the resurrection and the life, saith the Lord.'

The sun was warm; across the bright green fairway we could see the waves sparkling in the beautiful sweep of the bay; there was no thwack of golf balls; all was still. We walked forward beneath the shadow of the lych gate and towards the little church. Then we noticed that Bonnie was not following. The dog, usually attached to my heels by invisible elastic, was lurking the other side of the lych gate, stock still.

'Bonnie, come!' we called.

She held back.

'*Bonnie, come!*' – more imperious now.

Still no movement.

I walked back and chivvied her along – and it was then that Robin and I glanced at each other in astonishment. Clearly, the little dog did not want to walk past the coffin stone. Her tail and head were down. She pressed herself to the wall in that narrow space – too well-trained to dis-obey me yet full of fear – slinking past the resting place of the dead, giving the stone as wide a berth as possible.

It was extraordinary. What could a dog sense in a chunk of stone that had been there for centuries? There could not possibly be any smell of dead people for her sensitive nose to pick up, no physical manifestation of mortality. But still she slunk uneasily, as if she knew something, as if affected by the dead souls whose black-clad families had followed the coffins to that spot over centuries, heads bent, faces full of grief.

Once she had traversed the frightening shadow under the lych gate, she darted up the path to the church porch as if nothing had happened. Later, when we left the tiny church and strolled around the churchyard and paid homage at Betjeman's grave, it was time to walk back to the beach. I wondered then if I should be kind and pick Bonnie up. But we were curious to see if her demonstration of fear had been a fluke. It had not. She behaved in exactly the same way, cringing away from the lych stone, then trotting off across the bright green sward of the golf course, as if relieved to leave the nameless thing behind.

I do not find it unbelievable that Sophie tuned in to the spirit of Bonnie that day, just as Bonnie herself had sensed those disturbing vibrations from the dead in the lych gate of St Enodoc. There is – quite simply – no other explanation for the behaviour. We have no real understanding of what shimmers beyond the sphere of our crude consciousness, our hobbled intellects, our imperfect imaginations.

In very many cultures the dog has been seen as a guide between the worlds of the living and the dead. The dog may be a ferocious creature who guards the gates of hell, or a 'psychopomp' (a conductor of souls), attending the gods and guiding spirits to the land of the dead. When Goethe's hero Faust, consumed with despair at the emptiness of his life, prays to die and asks for a guide to 'distant lands', a stray black poodle appears and follows him home. The unhappy scholar is pleased to have a companion who will retrieve sticks and so on. Unfortunately the dog who has 'chosen' Faust happens to be Mephistopheles in disguise – which could be a pointed antecedent for the name that Churchill (and many others since) have given to that devil 'black dog' called depression. In *Faust*, Mephistopheles has the unhappy scholar's actual salvation as the ultimate goal, so the black dog can be (no matter how indirectly) a means to a good end.

And it could be that at the root of all those old stories about dogs as guides is the knowledge that the animal that became essential to humankind in the late Palae-olithic Age (perhaps around 15,000 BC) will always be able to guide us to places we do not know, and help us through darkness that would otherwise be terrifying. Cer-tain aboriginal tribes in Australasia and the American continent have a traditional belief that spirits are only visible to highly gifted shamans or medicine men – and to dogs.

These are not issues of 'right' or 'wrong'. As T. S. Eliot wrote, 'All our knowledge brings us nearer to our igno-rance.' My dog's death had set me thinking about the role of animals in my own life and what I had learned from them – and was still learning. I wanted to read, to study, to understand – even if that process brought me no closer to any sort of explanation of all that had happened since Bonnie's death. To me it felt momentous – and one effect was to make me think I knew nothing at all, and was therefore incapable of writing the kind of opinion article for my newspaper that once tripped so easily from my fingertips. Writing an advice column exposes you to the mystery at the heart of all human relationships, and there too, you increasingly see no 'right' and 'wrong' – unless physical and mental cruelty is involved. But to opine about political and social issues with the absolute conviction required by a tabloid newspaper? I cannot do it any more. One small white dog was reminding me that, in fact, we humans know nothing about the mists that rise from the fields at night and wreath around our houses.

Most pet lovers know about the story of 'The Rainbow Bridge'. A few years before Bonnie died I took some people to task on Facebook for sneering at this story (sometimes called a poem), which is used to help those who are inconsolable at the death of a pet. They called it sentimental and made fun of its saccharine certainty. 'Kitsch' was a word somebody used. I dislike such intellectual superiority and pointed out that if it *helps* then it is as valid as any of the myths, legends or folk tales which have assisted men, women and children to imagine other lives as well as gaining insight into their own.

It seems to me that the simple little late-twentieth-century construct (there are two or three suggestions for who wrote it, but nobody seems to know for sure) is actually very interesting, and relates directly to the ancient and cross-cultural idea of animals as guides. Here it is, in full:

There is a bridge connecting heaven and earth. It is called the Rainbow Bridge because of its many colours. Just this side of the Rainbow Bridge there is a land of meadows, hills and valleys with lush green grass.

When a beloved pet dies, the pet goes to this place. There is always food and water and warm spring weather. All the animals who have been ill and old are restored to health and vigour; those who were hurt or maimed are made whole and strong again, just as we remember them in our dreams of days and times gone by.

The animals are happy and content, except for one small thing; they each miss someone very special to them, who had to be left behind. They all run and play together, but the day comes when one suddenly stops and looks into the distance. Her bright eyes are intent; her eager body begins to quiver. Suddenly she begins to run from the group, flying over the green grass, her legs carrying her faster and faster. You have been spotted, and when you and your special friend finally meet, you cling together in

joyous reunion. The happy kisses rain upon your face;
your hands again caress the beloved head, and you look
once more into the trusting eyes of your pet, so long gone
from your life but never absent from your heart.

Then you cross the Rainbow Bridge together, never again
to be separated.

The most important thing to note is that the green
meadow is located this side of heaven. This beautiful
place is not heaven itself (although all the pets are having a good time there) but is the portal to paradise. I shall
return to this idea, and the issue of the soul (animal and
human), later in this book – for now what interests me
is that in 'The Rainbow Bridge' the pets wait specifically
to act as guides to their humans. That is their role – and
this is as important as the joy of reunion. It is the animals
who take the humans across the bridge to heaven – as if
the strength of the relationship between them is what
provides the energy for the journey.

The idea of the bridge between worlds is itself very
ancient. In old Norse mythology, Bifröst is a burning rainbow bridge that reaches between Midgard (the world)
and Asgard (the realm of the gods). This is written in the

collection of writings called the Poetic Edda, compiled in the thirteenth century from much earlier sources. In Persian mythology a bridge spans the gulf between heaven and earth, impossible for the wicked to cross but easy for good souls. There are many other descriptions and pictures of similar bridges in medieval manuscripts across Europe, and in all cases it is not the skill of the soul but its quality, its condition, that allows it to cross the bridge. So the modern folk tale (for want of a better term) of the Rainbow Bridge may seem silly but it evokes much older beliefs. Any animal lover will see that it is good people – those who have cared for their pets – who are rewarded with eternal devotion matching the loyalty displayed on earth. They are the ones who will be led to paradise by their cats and dogs, over the Rainbow Bridge.

I needed to look at Bonnie's ashes. In two months I hadn't done so, and the thought filled me with fear. When you bury your pet, he is in the earth and there is no need to see or touch any part again. But when you have the ashes, what will happen to them? One of my friends sourced a particular jar from India, and now it stands in her sitting room on a low table. 'That way I can feel my dog is always with me, as he was in life.' Another friend told me that the cremation urn containing her dog's ashes 'sits on the living-room windowsill, so she can watch people going past'.

Bonnie's ashes were still sealed in the carton handed to us; I kept them in a battered Victorian box, together with her brush, a kerchief bearing the initial B, her paw prints, and all the cards kind people sent when she died. From time to time I got them out, read every one, and cried. One day Sophie looked at me anxiously as I was doing this and stood up, her paws on my knees. When I picked her up she licked my face all over, tasting my tears, just as Bonnie had tasted them in the seconds before her heart stopped beating. I explained to Sophie how I was feeling and told her I couldn't help it. Those liquid brown Chihuahua eyes seemed to jump out of her head in understanding.

I had read that people whose pets have been cremated sometimes worry that the ashes they are handed back may not be the 'right' remains. How do they know? To find out I decided to return to Companions Haven and talk to the person who had cremated my dog, the last human being to touch her. It felt important to be sure it had been done with tenderness.

So I telephoned Kelly Pawsey, a former BBC employee (blest with a surname perfect for someone who loves animals), and went back to where I had last seen Bonnie in her earthly form. It was a beautiful day at the end of winter and Kelly and I sat in her large comfortable kitchen, across the garden from the little 'chapel of rest' used by those who bring their pets.

She and her husband Mike bought the pet crematorium in 2012 when they were looking for a home in an area north-west of Bath and near Bristol. They found a house they liked, but it happened to be attached to a thriving business of a sort only a special kind of person would want to take on. Not many would want a cremation oven in their garden, even if it was one designed for animals. Companions Haven was established in Pucklechurch, Gloucestershire, by Josephine and Robert Carlyle in May 1991, and was a founder member of the Association of Private Pet Cemeteries and Crematoria (APPCC), established in 1993 to set standards for the industry. Kelly Pawsey is at pains to explain to me that they are inspected yearly by the Animal Health

Veterinary Laboratories Agency and hold a pet cremation licence issued by the Environment Agency. This is
all very important. There have been horror stories you do
not want to think about when, choosing cremation, you
hand over your pet's body to a stranger.

Kelly believes you have to be an animal lover to do
the work. She and her assistants Sally and Jackie certainly are:

> ... although obviously you have to get used to handling
> dead animals and develop a degree of detachment. But
> empathy is essential. People can feel very embarrassed
> about their feelings and mumble, 'I know it's just a dog'
> or 'I know it's just a cat' or sometimes they feel angry; our
> job is to make sure they can say goodbye in the best pos-
> sible way, and handle our part in that process well. We
> take care of every kind of pet, from a Crufts winner to a
> scruffy mutt from the animal shelter to a precious prize cat
> to a little gerbil or rabbit. We have to deal with older peo-
> ple, who have become disabled, losing a companion and
> helper dog, which can be so very hard. And sometimes I
> find the men get very emotional. I always remember one
> guy – it was early on, so it sticks in my mind – who was

a very big bloke and brought his cat in her basket. All around her he had carefully placed twenty-four red roses. And he was desperately upset, holding this cat and the flowers in the basket. I remember it so well.

Kelly tells me of the Hindu families who decorate the chapel with tinsel and little effigies of one or two of their gods, then wait and stand in the lane outside, so they can see the smoke rising from the cremation oven. She recalls people bringing favourite blankets, toys, collars, bowls, even letters to their pets. Sometimes it quickly becomes obvious to her that within the grief for the dead pet is wrapped another grief: 'A lot of people will say, "My dad died a few months ago" or "I got divorced last year" or "Now I'm this age, well, I won't get another dog, you see." It can be heart-breaking.'

If a pet dies at the vet, she explains, they should be told that 'disposal' can be 'common' or 'individual'. An individual cremation will obviously cost more as Kelly and the team make absolutely sure that the oven is swept out spotlessly, the only ashes left being that one pet's. But when a cheaper common cremation happens, 'we scatter the ashes on our flower beds here, and people do come on the anniversary of the death and walk in the gardens and remember'.

We talk about her own dogs, and as she remembers them her eyes fill with tears.

You see them around the home, don't you? In the corner of the eye? They're there for a while and then they go. Yes, people have asked me the question of whether an animal has a spirit. They can't believe their dog is dead because he looks as though he is sleeping, with his head just poking around the blanket. They worry that the soul is still there ... So we often show them the Rainbow Bridge story, because it's comforting for them, to think of being welcomed there, you know? Do I believe it? Ohhh ... I don't know. My pet has been an important part of my journey and that's enough. I just enjoy remembering what was.

It is one of those days when you can sense the end of winter in the green shoots pushing through the soil, and the daffodils are gilded by clear, crisp sunlight. January the 30th; I have invited the family for the unveiling of Bonnie's memorial plaque. The letter-cutter and sculptor Iain Cotton delivered it two days earlier, exactly to my design, capturing the leaping enthusiasm of an illustration by Sarah McMenemy (from my 'Bonnie' series), translated into carved slate. No need for any fancy inscription; just the image, the name, the dates and a little cross. Robin fixes it fairly low on a wall within the walled garden and we cover it with a cloth, held down by stones. Then we plant dwarf daffodils in bloom in a cluster underneath, leaving space for something…

At last I steel myself to open the carton and take hold of the plastic bag containing Bonnie's ashes. Such a soft grey. Such tiny grains. Such a pitiful pile of what was once a sweet, loving little dog. *Is that really it?*

Carefully I tip some of the ashes into a little box, and into the ground they go, together with a crystal heart a friend gave me when Bonnie died. Then it is time for the family to assemble at 12.30, as bid. They line up on the path, opposite the veiled plaque. Robin and I stand each side of the cloth, and I look at the faces of my parents, my children, their spouses and their children, while three dogs, Freddie, Dotty and little Sophie, roam around behind them. The two three-year-olds have very different demeanours. Barnaby is suitably solemn, and clings to his mother, who has explained what the event is about. Chloe looks inquisitive, like someone who will always take charge.

I make a short speech, directed at the children, telling them that when a pet dies we feel very, very unhappy and miss them so much because we loved them, but it is so important to remember the happy times you had together. Looking directly at them I say, 'You know that when Bonnie died I felt very sad, didn't I?'

Chloe pipes up, 'Bonnie was sleeping on the table.' She remembers.

I then name everybody and say what Bonnie meant to them, even my son-in-law, who did not have a bond with the little dog, but respected mine. Unusually for me, there are no readings, because no fancy words are needed. All I need to do is proclaim that of course Bonnie will never be forgotten, then simultaneously Robin and I remove the stones and the cloth falls to the ground and there is Bonnie, leaping into our shared sunlight.

Everybody claps and Dotty, Freddie and Sophie look up at the unexpected noise.

After the slate memorial is duly admired, the children especially liking the picture and saying, 'Bonnie!', it is time to go inside to toast her and eat the lunch that awaits in the oven. As we drift towards the house my son watches his svelte chocolate Labrador as she follows the others through the garden door. Quietly he murmurs to me that this has all made him think. 'We got Dotty when we all came to the farm so she's six already…'

How *short* is the life of a dog. ⚘

CHAPTER EIGHT

A dog can never tell you what she knows from the
smells of the world, but you know, watching her,
that you know
almost nothing.

From 'Her Grave' by Mary Oliver (b. 1935)

C HARLES DARWIN WAS convinced that dogs have feelings. He noted: 'I have seen a dog doing what he ought not to do and looking ashamed of himself.' Every dog lover will recognise that, while cat lovers will offer feline cool as proof of superiority.

The man who challenged and changed human thinking with *On the Origin of Species* observed that dogs communicate with different sounds and 'laugh for joy', that they are 'unselfish' and have a sense of humour, a feeling for time and free will. In *The Descent of Man* he points out that although dogs may have lost some of the natural cunning of their ancestors, the wolves and jackals, 'yet they have progressed in certain moral qualities, such as affection, trust-worthiness, temper and probably in general intelligence'.

Moral qualities? All those ideas would have been as controversial to his peers as to the later animal 'experts' and scientists who poured scorn on anthropomorphism. But a little later in *The Descent of Man*, in a very strange passage, Darwin seems to go a step further and attribute what might be called a spiritual awareness to his loved and respected canine companion. One hot day his dog was lying on the lawn, quite near an open parasol. Nobody was near this sunshade; if there had been (Darwin says) the dog would have ignored the occasional slight movements it made in a breeze because he would have assumed the human was causing them. 'As it was, every time that the parasol slightly moved, the dog growled fiercely and barked.' From this observation Darwin makes what most people will see as a bizarre and illogical leap – from a parasol to 'spiritual agencies'.

He guesses that his dog 'reasoned to himself in a rapid and unconscious manner' that the parasol was moving because of 'the presence of some strange living agent'. He then proceeds to talk about religion – and this is quite extraordinary: 'The feeling of religious devotion is a highly complex one, consisting of love, complete submission to an exalted and mysterious superior, a strong sense of dependence, fear, reverence, hope for the future…' Darwin believes that 'no being could experience so complex an emotion until advanced in his intellectual and moral faculties to at least a moderately high level'. (There is much to disagree with there, when we consider the deranged behaviour of some so-called believers nowadays, but he was writing in a very different age.)

Darwin believes that it was 'high mental faculties' that first led men 'to believe in unseen spiritual agencies'. Therefore it is all the more significant when he writes: 'We see some distant approach to this state of mind in the deep love of a dog for his master, associated with complete submission, some fear and perhaps other feelings.'

It seems as if the great scientist saw dogs and humans as travelling along the same path, with the humans just a little way ahead, and believed that both species are distinguished by a sense of the *other*. Rationalists may hate this, but I want to tap them on a shoulder on a very dark night when the wind is howling and the rain rattling eerily on the window pane, and whisper, 'Hey, people, admit it – some things are simply beyond reason.'

So I sit at home, thinking of the signs that followed the death of my pet, knowing I am not alone in my conviction that strange forces could be at work. If Darwin recorded the sympathy he witnessed in animal behaviour (not just dogs either) and attempts to give comfort, why should it be strange that Dotty should feel sorry for me because my dog was dead? Why should I not feel the physical presence of my dead dog, when a great scientist sought to find some sort of link between a parasol, an uneasy dog and spiritual feelings – a link, that is, between the seen and the unseen? All Darwin's scientific observation and research left him alive to *mystery* – and that fact encourages me. I have suffered persistent low-level ill-health since Bonnie's death; is it so strange therefore to surmise there was a deep spiritual bond between an intelligent grown woman and a funny little lapdog, which has actually survived her death and left me − literally − gasping for breath?

On a quest for answers I went to see Lisa Tenzin-Dolma, who is a novelist and non-fiction writer as well as a highly experienced clinical animal behaviourist, specialising in dogs. The founder and principal of the International School for Canine Behaviour and Psychology, Lisa is a slim, wiry woman with an infectious enthusiasm for life, surely caught from the many dogs she has treated. She easily passes my personal 'tail-wag' test for humans: that openness that defies cynicism and embraces vulnerability. She talked to me cheerfully about dogs she has treated − ones with massive aggression problems, fostered dogs with agoraphobia, uncontrollable dogs who leap on visitors, dogs who exhibit pitiful separation anxiety and fear, and dogs with obsessive-compulsive disorder who walk in endless circles, 'fly-snap' the air when there is nothing there, or lick their paws until they open up terrible sores.

Lisa is one of those rather heroic people who take in dogs that have been ill-treated, and is prepared to do all she can to give them a wonderful quality of life until they die, even if that is only a few months. For example, her first rescue greyhound, Orla, had been kept in a shed in Ireland with no natural light and made to have litter after litter until she was worn out with lack of food, breeding and ill-treatment. Orla was rescued and brought to England and when Lisa first took her home, the dog stood hesitantly on the threshold. She had never been inside a house before. 'Then her face lit up, as if to say, *I've come home.*' The dog recognised kindness, even though she had never met it before.

That poor greyhound died ten months later, and the night after her death Lisa's daughter Amber had a vivid dream that Orla was telling her she was at peace and happy. Lisa was distraught that she could not cure all the dog's multiple problems and bestow a longer time of happiness. But two months after Orla's death she appeared in a dream to Lisa too, telling her that she was 'well and happy and grateful for her time with us'.

Later, along came Shep, a collie–husky cross who had been shut up inside for twelve years. Lisa was tired at the time and wanted a break from fostering, because 'it's as if each dog who dies opens the wounds of all those who've died before'. But then a charity which specialises in rescuing elderly dogs called her to say they were desperate to find a home for Shep. How could she not say yes?

As we sat in her quiet sitting room, with Skye, her elderly and ailing deerhound–greyhound–saluki mix, snoozing on the floor between us, Lisa first used the word 'soul' – and I realised that I had been afraid to use it myself, even though it was what I wanted to talk about. 'There are certain dogs you have a powerful bond with,' she said. 'Those are your soulmate dogs – and Shep was one of those.'

'Like me and Bonnie,' I said.

'Exactly. It's a real connection as well as an intense love. It's as if you have known that animal for ever. As soon as I saw Shep I knew and he was the same. There was a recognition.'

But fifteen-year-old Shep was to have only three months of a miraculous new, happy life with Lisa.

He died one afternoon and I was devastated. I went to bed and cried myself to sleep. Now, because of his age Shep would need to go outside more than once in the middle of the night. I'd hear the scrabble of his claws on the wooden floor as he struggled to get up and I'd come down and let

him out into the garden. It was always a magical time at
2 a.m., with the sounds of owls and foxes. Even though it
was cold I didn't mind. The night he died I woke because
I heard his claws, and rushed downstairs, telling myself,
He's dead. For two weeks I heard him, every single night,
and came downstairs, and when I woke up each day it
was with this real feeling of love. It was as if his spirit
hadn't left, because of the strong love between us. It's as if
consciousness can go on existing after the body has died,
if there is a powerful enough bond. That's why some tribes
have ceremonies to draw the spirit onwards. Perhaps it is
our need that draws the consciousness (whether human or
animal) back, because they know we need comfort. But
then it fades ... and after about two weeks I did feel Shep's
spirit had finally gone.

The room was still. I could hear Skye breathing. It pleased
me to hear Lisa talk this way, because at last I felt able
to confide what I had only told Robin: how on that cold
December day I felt Bonnie's physical presence on my
bed, the nudge behind me, the feeling of her weight at
my back. She nodded as if this revelation was the most
natural thing in the world.

What's more, she had her own story of physical 'presence' to tell me. Her book *Charlie: The Dog Who Came In from the Wild* tells how in 2013 she took on a one-eyed, feral dog from Romania in what she calls 'the greatest canine challenge' of her life. Street-dog Charlie (the size of a large Labrador) was fierce, strong, traumatised and potentially very dangerous, which makes the story of the bond that developed between him, Lisa and Amber all the more moving. At the end of the book, Lisa describes how her dog sickened and died in spring 2015, and writes:

> *Charlie was the most extraordinary being I have ever known, and the void left by his passing is immense. The purity of his wild soul shone through him like a guiding light, and he taught me so much about how we humans seek to find ways to return to this natural state...*

Sitting at home one year later, Lisa told me something that isn't in her book.

> *Charlie was such a massive force in my life because he made me look not just at feral dogs' behaviour, but at*

issues of trust between animals and humans – and many other things. He actually made me very introspective and changed me… So when he died I felt I wouldn't get over it. I have my beautiful children and I have Skye – so how could I think like that? But Charlie was another soul-mate and all the more special because of what he had been through. Anyway, one day, I was sitting on the sofa, crying as I thought about him. Now Charlie used to sit curled around my legs; that was his favourite place. On this particular day, as I cried, I suddenly felt this warmth. It was like an electric shock, through my legs and my whole body. I knew it was Charlie. He'd come to comfort me. I could feel him: that electric current, in the shape – the space – where he used to be.

It is one thing to be told by many, many readers that they have had similar experiences; that was the case when the *Daily Mail* published my article about Bonnie. But it is much more moving to hear from somebody you know and respect – to hear face to face – that you are not alone. From time to time people would ask me whether or not I believe that animals have souls, but I turned aside from the question.

What was engaging me in these months (as I grew used to having Sophie in the house, knowing she could never replace Bonnie) was the idea that the physical sense of a dog (or a cat, but I no longer have any cat expertise) could linger – and what this implied. Of course the phenomena Lisa and I experienced could be 'explained' in terms of wishful thinking, straightforward neediness or over-active imaginations, but that would be to imply that we are dim, deluded or dishonest.

Yet that is not the case.

At this stage I considered consulting one of the mediums who claim to be able to contact dead animals and even did some research on the internet. The trouble is, I instinctively feel such people are charlatans, therefore what would I be trying to do? The journalist within me supplies the mischievous answer, 'Catch 'em out,' but while the experiment would certainly be interesting, I no longer have time for such games, nor do I wish a stranger to pretend to speak to me with the voice of my dead dog. The world is full of people who are ready to take money from the gullible and I want no part of it, although if somebody derives comfort from being told that Fido or Bessie is romping happily in a green field and sending messages back, then so be it.

Instead, I went to speak to another person who has devoted an entire career to working with animals, and for whom no aspect of their behaviour is a surprise. Sarah Fisher is the UK's highest-qualified equine and companion animal instructor. She runs the British office of TTouch, an extraordinary technique pioneered in the USA to help dogs (and other animals too) overcome health and behavioural issues using gentle exercises. Practitioners must have a detailed knowledge of an animal's nervous system and understand communication and animal responses like fear or flight. When I first heard of Sarah, some years ago, she was described to me as a 'horse whisperer'. This was somebody I would be able to talk to.

I went to meet her at the TTouch headquarters, on a farm near Bath. She was disappointed I had failed to bring the little rescue dog I'd told her about in my email, and I realised I had missed an opportunity to have Sophie assessed by an expert. When you adopt a rescue dog you know they might be bringing emotional (that word again) baggage you can only guess at, but the foxy little creature seemed to be settling in well…

Warm, tousled and passionate, Sarah Fisher lost no time in announcing her conviction that animals, especially dogs, operate on a plane most people do not understand. 'They have a soul,' she said, 'without a doubt.' There it was – at the beginning of the conversation, although I had not raised the vexed question. Day after day I shied away from the thought that Bonnie had a soul and that the fine, dancing entity was still with me. The thought was too much. But I wanted it to be true.

Sarah explained that she has lived with animals all her life, has worked closely with them for twenty years, and is convinced that they have much to teach us – more than we realise.

We train them how to function in our world, but they are teaching us too. Something of the glory of animals touches us – if we are receptive to it. This is a knowledge which, once you have it, you cannot unlearn. Cats are solitary but they teach us too – to move in small increments. They are the supreme hunters and can climb high, literally and figuratively. Every animal is here to teach us something.

I loved the humility of that statement. Humankind is arrogant and believes it knows everything and has the right to plunder the earth. The older I become, the more I hate this, and the less I trust my own species. As Sarah poured coffee into chunky mugs I recalled one dead fledgling and one dead otter pup and gave thanks for lessons I did not, at the time, know I was receiving.

As Sarah Fisher's love and respect for animals tumbled out I felt in the presence of a kindred spirit. She told me of a time when she had to go to Poland to teach, even though one of her dogs had been ill and she had just heard that surgery for a tumour was needed. Sick at heart, she left. Then one night, in her hotel, she dreamed that the dog had died. So she telephoned her husband and told him he had to go to the vet as soon as he could because instinct (or animal communication?) was warning her. But although he could be there, he could not change what was about to happen.

> I was in this hotel room crying and crying, when I suddenly stopped and felt a white light go through me. I later discovered that was the moment my dog died... We had such a connection. I actually felt her.

Then there was that certain knowledge that she had gone.

She paused, and her eyes filled with tears as she said, 'You know, Bel, we mustn't stop sharing these moments because we are afraid people will laugh. We must be courageous.'

I talked a little about Bonnie, and how the sadness (unspoken now) will not leave me. Sarah explained that in her experience a companion animal's death is the precursor of something that will happen in your life. A shift.

I've seen this pattern; an incredible animal leaves you and you're left feeling hollow, but what you don't know is, you're being moved on to the next stage. At the point of their death there is hope – because they have done what they can for you, and it is your privilege to be at the parting. Wherever I go and whatever I do all my dogs are with me all the time, and I trust them to send me the next one.

This was the perfect cue for me to tell this stranger the story of my dream of Happy Landings, and then the photograph that seemed to move. Of course none of it surprised her. Bonnie had led me to Sophie? Of course. In Sarah Fisher's animal world it would be a given that Sophie was 'sent'. And now the person who is an expert in what might be called a 'laying on of hands' to cure animals of mental and physical problems, turned to counsel me.

Of course you grieve when your dog dies – you must grieve. But you know, when an animal dies I don't believe it's the end. You go through the pain, and think you can't do it again, all the loss… but you can. Their passing reminds me of the perfect rhythm of life, and in that sense I have no regrets at the shortness of the time we have together. You have shared a sort of perfection: the love, the connection, the learning. That realisation helps with the grief. I just give thanks that I have been able to be in harmony with that amazing dance the animals have taught me. They are beautiful beings, sent to teach us – and then they leave us behind. And they leave us changed for the better.

When you choose to love a pet you welcome pain into your heart, because, in the natural order of events, the animal is destined to die first. This must be borne. I had learned this already, yet those conversations helped me to realise that if 'every man's death diminishes me' (in the words of John Donne's great meditation when Dean of St Paul's), so the death of a beloved animal ought to be allowed to enlarge me. And by that token (to challenge Donne outright, who told us in the same meditation that 'no man is an island') *any* death can enlarge – oh yes, even the pain, the grief, the loss, the mourning, the anguish. All of it, for human or animal. But only if the love is so great that it can, in the end, carry the sorrow onwards, as a snowball rolls downhill, growing larger all the while. I have spent over forty years writing (from time to time, but regularly) about bereavement and yet mourning my little dog has taught me as much as any of the books I have read.

🐕 🐕 🐕 🐕

Bonnie's ashes were in the old box, with her brush (still holding her white hairs), the cards etc. – and my memories crammed into a wooden coffin of their own, crammed so tight they might burst the lid. But now it was time to think of something else to do with what I had left of her. Lisa Tenzin-Dolma keeps Charlie's ashes in a handsome urn in her sitting room, but that was not for me. I believe in symbols, in memorials, but what to do? The physical remains of the dead matter. When you consign flesh to the earth, whether human or animal, you have somewhere to go, to mourn, to think, to remember. A plastic bag of grey ashes has no poetry. Imagination is required.

When I took Bonnie's photograph, the night she died, I could not have explained that action. Sometimes you act according to pre-ordained impulses – some folk memory bubbling to the surface, some need for ritual that flows in the blood. When the art of photography became commonplace it was inevitable that people would wish every aspect of their lives to be recorded, from their dogs to their dead. In 2011 Audrey Linkman published her strange and enthralling book, *Photography and Death*. It collects and analyses the post-mortem portraits which are an all-but-forgotten part of domestic history in the nineteenth century. Here are agonising pictures of babies posed artfully as if asleep, a woman holding her dead babies, children standing around the deathbed of a sibling, and a particularly poignant image of a girl who looks about ten, propped sitting in a chair surrounded by her dolls.

Why would people do that? In those far-off days there wasn't the narcissistic wish to record every bat of an eyelash or pout of a mouth that we are (unfortunately) so familiar with today. There was also, surely, for most people, a sense of the sacred – of God's purpose and an afterlife – which ought to have rendered memorial pictures unnecessary. Yet of course it did not. The flesh was ephemeral and heaven eternal; nevertheless people clung to what they had, a wistful longing that the beloved dead were only sleeping and should be recorded as such. The photographs that resulted were tokens that shouted defiantly, 'This person was here with us, even for a short time,' in the face of that old Grim Reaper, with his stink of the charnel house. So, at a time when children (although many of the pictures are of adults too) would be taken all too soon by illness, people took photographs, posed carefully, to mimic life.

How interesting that my instinct prompted that very action with Bonnie, arranging her as though she were asleep, and taking the pictures that I still keep in my smartphone. Reading Linkman's book again, I came across another passage: 'Flowers were the most widely used accessory appearing in portraits of males, females and children … Scattered on the deathbed flowers served as tokens of the survivors' love for their dead and as evidence of their concern to take proper, reverent care of the body.' An image flashed into my mind: Kelly Pawsey's memory of a big man grieving as he carried his dead cat for cremation, with the twenty-four red roses lovingly placed just so, all around the animal.

People like that man are wise not to be ashamed, not to accept the 'just a dog' or 'just a cat' philosophy. Is it to make too much of an animal's death, to want to memorialise? Sarah Fisher shook her head and told me, in no uncertain terms, 'I feel sorry for people who dismiss these feelings and say, "Only a *dog*" … Honestly, I pity them.' As I write that, I smile to myself, knowing that a large number of people will pity *us* – we who mourn our pets so much. So be it.

The philosopher Alain de Botton writes (in *Art as Therapy*): 'Art helps us accomplish a task that is of central importance in our lives: to hold on to things we love when they have gone.' This is precisely the point of those photographs of the dead, of the act of choosing a beautiful urn for ashes, and of the mourning jewellery that was so popular with the Victorians and Edwardians, which usually incorporated the hair of the beloved dead. You may find this dark, morbid, even repellent, but I do not. On the contrary, such things accept the reality of death but are determined to seize a little permanence in defiance. And in everlasting love.

'Did you know you could have Bonnie's ashes made into a piece of jewellery?' somebody suggested on Facebook. It was an interesting idea, but when I looked at websites I could not feel very enthusiastic about the pieces on offer. Jewellery is so personal; Bonnie's hair plaited into a Victorian mourning ring would have suited me better, but that was impossible. So I planned to drive about 160 miles (because my research led me to a firm called Ashes into Glass in Billericay, Essex) to have some fragments of her ashes incorporated into a necklace ... but there was no need. I discovered that I could have the same thing done in Bath, just six miles from our home, by a company called Bath Aqua Glass, whose showroom I had walked past with Bonnie many times.

Here's what I read on the website:

Our Memorial Glass range creatively encapsulates a loved one or pet animal's cremation ashes into glass. Timeless and beautiful, our Memorial Glass jewellery and keepsakes can be cherished & passed down through the generations. By incorporating a small amount of cremation ashes into a piece of handblown or fused glass, we can create jewellery and keepsakes that can be forever treasured. We offer this service with respect, love and understanding. We only use a small amount of cremation ashes (less than one level teaspoon per piece) therefore we can create mixed/matched sets for the whole family to cherish. All Memorial Glass pieces can be engraved using our in-house engraving service ... All our glass is Lead-Free and can therefore be held or worn next to the skin without issue.

This was the way forward. I would have some of Bonnie's ashes made into a paperweight to sit on my desk. This would be my version of a reliquary. In Christianity and Buddhism a reliquary is a container for relics – fragments of the 'true cross' or of saints' bones. Many times have

I pored over these beautiful objects in museums; now a portion of my little dog would be blown into glass to fulfil a similar function, not worship of course, but remembrance, and 'to hold on to things we love after they have gone'.

Looking online I saw what anxiety the process of turning ashes into a glass object can cause the bereft people who consider it. 'How will I know the ashes are actually my mother's?' is a typical question – reminding me of that same anxiety over cremated remains. Are they the right ones? This matters very much; the ashes are as sacred as any relics that were placed in medieval reliquaries, and certainly more authentic.

I wanted to witness the whole process in order to be able to endorse it for others. So I requested a special dispensation from Bath Aqua Glass, to be assured that it is done with scrupulous care. So one chilly day I take the plastic bag of Bonnie's ashes from my keepsake box and drive to Bath, then walk to my appointment – all the way up Walcot Street, where we used to walk, Bonnie prancing on one of her coloured leads.

Judith Devereux is the person in charge of this very special aspect of the glass company's work, which they have only been offering for three or four years. 'We get such a lot of feedback from people who say how comforting they find it – possessing an object, whatever they choose, made with the ashes.' She tells me she is going to take me through the process as if I were somebody who had sent for their information pack online.

So, a form is filled in, and a spoonful of ashes is placed into a little plastic bag, carefully labelled with my name, and then clipped to the sheet, the whole then being placed in a labelled plastic sleeve. 'It all has to be logged,' explains Judith, 'so there's no chance at all of ashes being mixed up. We have to be very meticulous, as this matters so much to people.'

Then she introduces me to Ian and Harry, who will be in charge of my paperweight. These two young men tell me they take the task very seriously, and that the memorial pieces are only made on one day of the week. I have a sense of pleasing reverence. 'This is a two-person job,' says Harry, 'because I'm in charge of the paperwork from start to finish, everything carefully logged – you just can't get ashes muddled – while Ian will be shaping the glass.'

Bonnie's ashes (such a small amount…) are sieved on to
a small, spotless metal stand. Then everything seems
to happen very quickly, as I stand watching, too mes-
merised by the process to take proper notes. A blob of
molten glass on the end of a rod, glowing, the end coated
in my chosen colour. It is dipped into Bonnie's ashes on
the metal surface, picking up only the dusting required.
Behind Ian, the mouth of the furnace is incandescent,
like the maw of hell. He sits, wearing dark glasses against
all this heat and light, takes a pair of pincers and twists

the molten blob at arm's length, so that Bonnie's ashes are carried all through in a spiral. Then this has to be encased in molten glass ... and I feel bewildered, because the explanations ('Now it has to be soaked to equalise') go over my head. All I can focus on is that blazing blob, which now contains part of my little dog and which will cool, in a few days, to a blue paperweight for my desk.

Bonnie is glowing at 600 degrees. She is placed to cool in a tray of mica. She flares in shades of red and green that will cool in time to blue, but look now like a mini-globe, a world that holds the colours of Australia's wild places, flaring orange-scarlet and lush green. Dazed, I can feel the radiance of her heat, just three feet away from me. It makes me want to cry. But the guys are talking to me helpfully about the technicalities of the process, and I must seem to listen...

What matters is the care they took, and that Bonnie is now swirling in her own small planet, soon to be put aside in a special cooling cupboard, for the heat slowly to wane over days. Then my paperweight will be ready for engraving with a single letter, B. I am almost speech-less when they hand me the remaining ashes to carry home once more, then painstakingly clean the table top, ready for the next ashes – the next sorrow to be caught in glass.

I feel something miraculous has happened.

One week later I go to collect the piece, and buy two hand-blown champagne glasses while I am at the show-room. Bonnie will be toasted yet again. At home Robin and I slowly unwrap the box together and I lift out the memorial object. 'That's beautiful,' he says, his face expressing something of the awe I feel.

Oh, you do not have to tell me this is only a *paper-weight*. Nothing more or less than a pretty glass orb in two shades of turquoise blue, engraved with an elegant B, complete with serifs. This is no reliquary, no sacred object... One day maybe, when I am dead, the object will end up in a charity shop, to be bought for a song by some-body called Barbara or Bernadette who loves the colour, and cannot know those scattered grains are the ashes of a small white dog.

Yet when I pick up my paperweight and turn it slowly, to follow the spiral swirls of ash suspended in an infinity of blue, it is like holding a whole galaxy in the palm of my hand. When I raise it to my eyes, with light behind, I could be looking into ocean eddies, when the sunlight reaches down to illuminate a myriad minute fragments of shell, caught in the currents, swirling forever and ever. When I lift it to my forehead the glass is cold but soothing and bids headaches disappear. If I close my eyes and trace the outline of the B, slightly rough to the touch, I can see Bonnie in my mind's eye – so pleased that, sharing the initial, the two of us are made one within this small thing of beauty.

CHAPTER NINE

Do you know that I believe that the first
to come and greet me when I go to heaven
will be this dear, faithful old
friend, Carlo?

Emily Dickinson (1830–86)

So one pooch says to another, 'Of course all dogs go to heaven – because we're not the ones who screwed up!' Or, as the bishop said, 'You must always remember that as far as the Bible is concerned, God only threw the humans out of Paradise.' Well, of course. No dog worthy of the name would listen to a snake or be keen to chomp on an *apple*.

Anyway, animals are innocent spirits. The internet is awash with jokes and anecdotes implying that they – especially dogs – have an afterlife, and I lap them up, like a happy cat with cream. When Bonnie died, more than one Facebook contact kindly sent me a famous *New Yorker* cartoon by Charles Barsotti. It shows clouds and a benign St Peter leaning nonchalantly on heaven's reception desk. The new arrival on the left is a balding man in late middle age, with no clothes and a look of sheer amazement on his face. Because bounding over the clouds towards him from the other side is a little dog, stubby tail wagging madly, mouth agape with soppy love. And the saint says, 'So you're little Bobbie; well, Rex here has been going on and on about you for the last fifty years.'

That old, endless love and fidelity can break your heart. Yet, of course, faithfulness is a two-way street, for (to paraphrase the Beatles) surely you take back the amount of love that you make. My favourite dog-and-heaven story is about such *human* devotion:

A man and his dog were walking along a road. The man was enjoying the scenery, when it suddenly occurred to him that he was dead. He remembered dying, and also realised that the pet walking beside him had been dead for years. Years before him. Dazed, he wondered where the road was leading them.

After a while, they came to a high, white stone wall along one side of the road, looking like fine marble. It ran up a long hill, where it was broken by a tall arch that glowed in the sunlight. The man was standing before a magnificent gate that glittered like mother-of-pearl, and the path to the gate shone like pure gold. Hot and tired, he walked with the dog at his heels towards the gate and saw a man sitting at a desk to one side. So he called out, 'Excuse me, where are we?'

'This is heaven,' came the reply.

'Wow! Would you happen to have some water?' the man asked.

'Of course, sir. Come right in, and I'll have some iced water brought to you.' He gestured, and immediately the magnificent gates began to open.

Pointing to his animal companion, the man asked, 'Can my dog come in, too?'

The guardian of the gate shook his head. 'I'm sorry, sir, but we don't accept pets.'

At that, the man thought a moment and then turned back towards the road and plodded on the way he had been going, with his thirsty dog beside him. After another long walk and at the top of another long hill, he came to a dirt road leading through a farm gate that looked as if it had never been closed. There was no fence. As he approached the gate, he saw a man inside, leaning against a tree and reading a book.

'Excuse me!' he called to the man. 'Do you have any water?'

'Yeah, sure, there's a pump over there, come on in.'

'How about my friend here?' the traveller said, bending to stroke his dog.

'Of course! You'll find a bowl by the pump.'

So the man and the dog went through the gate, and sure enough, there was an old-fashioned hand pump with a pet bowl beside it. The traveller took a long drink and filled the bowl for the dog.

Then they both walked back towards the man by the tree.

'What do you call this place?' the traveller asked.

'Why, this is heaven!' came the reply.

'Well, that's confusing,' said the traveller, 'because the man down the road said that was heaven, too.'

'Oh, you mean the place with the gold path and pearly gates? Oh no – that's hell.'

Puzzled, the man asked, 'But doesn't it make you angry that they use your name like that?'

The saint (for surely this was St Peter?) smiled and said, 'No, we're just happy that they screen out the people willing to leave their best friends behind.'

Cat lovers are welcome to recycle that story, replacing the dog with a cat, and there's no reason why the man shouldn't be riding on the precious pony he had as a child. Or maybe carrying the pet bunny that delighted him so much on his tenth birthday. Why not? The moral fable hinges on loyalty a human being can feel towards an animal – an emotion those of us who have been knocked sideways by pet bereavement understand only too well.

If the old accusation of sentimentality comes up, I refer the doubter to one of the greatest classics of world literature – which contains the same message. The Mahabharata is an epic of ancient India, written in Sanskrit and incorporating the famous Bhagavad Gita, probably written down around 400 BC, although much older in origin. My paperback copy is a hefty brick; the Mahabharata is the longest poem ever written. The unbelievably complicated plot about the adventures and trial of the Pandava brothers need not concern us here; what matters is that this is a profoundly moral story.

After a terrible war the brothers are left alive and decide to renounce worldly things. Clad in skins and rags they retire to the mountains and climb towards heaven in their bodily form. 'The righteous one' is called Yudhishthira and he leads four brothers, the princess Draupadi and 'the seventh companion … a dog that turned up to travel with them'. One by one each of the five companions weakens, stumbles and falls. Each time, Yudhishthira gives the reason for their demise: a sin or human failing, like pride. In the end only the virtuous Yudhishthira, who had tried everything to prevent the recent carnage, is left walking onwards, the stray dog at his side. Suddenly the 'thousand-eyed god' Indra appears in a glittering chariot and invites our hero to hop in for a ride to heaven. When the good king worries about leaving behind all his beloved fallen companions he is assured that they have gone to heaven before him.

Then here comes the Big Test. The noble warrior says, 'This dog is constant in his devotion to me. Let him go with me, for I feel a kindness towards him.'

Indra points out that the hero will now enjoy immortality and fame, but he must 'abandon the dog – there is no unkindness in this'. He warns Yudhishthira against being 'senseless'. The to-and-fro argument continues but the hero refuses to leave the dog behind, proclaiming, 'Let me not gain a glory for which I have to abandon a creature devoted to me.'

Then comes the dire warning: 'Dog owners have no place in heaven ... so think before acting ... and abandon the dog. There is no unkindness in this.' But Yudhish-thira will not have it. Invoking the noblest lessons of morality he argues, 'Abandoning one who is devoted is seen as a sin in the world ... Therefore I shall certainly not abandon him.'

Imagine the scene. You have the terrifying Lord of the Gods 'making heaven and earth resound with the roar of his chariot', warning the bedraggled, traumatised man not to be 'senseless', because he is assured of eternal glory alongside all the gods – if only he will leave the mutt behind. So what's wrong with you, human? Yet again, Yudhishthira flatly refuses, insisting that it would be a mortal sin to 'abandon one who is devoted'.

Now comes the great moment – the reward, the end of the quest, the transformation. For at that point the scruffy old stray dog changes into his true self: the Lord Yama, who represents the path of righteousness. Hooray! This shining creature 'delightedly' addresses the human 'in soft tones':

> You are of noble birth, with your father's intelligence,
> good conduct and compassion towards all beings ... You
> have given up a chariot to heaven because a mere dog is

*devoted to you. For this, lord of men, no one in heaven
is equal to you. Therefore … you have attained the high-
est celestial state.*

No pet owners in heaven? No pets? Then of course we
have no wish to go there, but will head off for the pagan
green fields and that Rainbow Bridge instead. Or I will
frolic in the clouds above the Himalayas with my little
dog and Sarama, the mother of all dogs. Alongside us
will be a whole herd of sacred cows, and Hanuman the
monkey god and elephant-headed Ganesha – the one
who, among his multifarious tasks, looks after writers.

The Hindu scriptures, myths and legends say that animals have souls – and therefore they occupy an important
place in Hinduism. You see them in Hindu art, as decora-
tion or as objects or worship – incarnations of gods and
goddesses. Every living being, from the animals down to
the insects, possesses a soul. Like humans, they are subject to the laws of nature and the cycle of birth and death
and possess their own special intelligence. According to
various schools of Hinduism, there is no spiritual distinc-
tion between human beings and other life forms, because
they are all manifestations of God – beings with souls.

Animals are not inferior creatures, but manifestations of God on the lower scale of evolution compared to man, each containing a spark of the divine, capable of becoming human and achieving salvation like the rest of us.

So is it surprising that a stray dog should prove to be the greatest moral test for a great and noble warrior, and that the loyal animal should, in the end, show its god-like form and be worthy of heaven? As I grow older I am more and more open to such ideas, not as literal truths but as metaphors for aspects of life and death, body and soul, that we cannot possibly *know*. One November I should like to make a pilgrimage to Nepal for Tihar, their version of Diwali, the festival of lights, which honours different creatures: crows, dogs, cows, oxen. The second day, Kukur Tihar, is the day dedicated to dogs, celebrating their role in human life. All dogs (to every last stray) are given food and draped with garlands (*malla*) as a mark of respect, and a red mark (the *tika*) is applied to each doggy forehead in a single stroke up from the eyes. This mark signals that the animal is a devotee of the righteous path and an object of devotion – even if only for one day. Tihar honours dogs in all their aspects, as guards, helpers, companions and friends, and the celebration is an acknowledgement of the deep connection between all living things.

Ah, but at the same time, neglect and terrible cruelty is the fate of countless dogs across the Indian subcontinent, and everywhere in the world, all year round. It is, you might say, all very well to drape hapless animals with garlands on one special day and then ignore them the rest of the time. What has such ritual treatment to do with the special bond between an individual human being and his or her companion animal? Nothing at all. Yet surely we can respond to colour and symbolism, keeping our minds open to poetry?

When Bonnie died I found myself obsessively reading about animals in other cultures, as if seeking confirmation for my feelings. I wondered whether a creature so loved could *not* have an essence which remains after death and perhaps even connects to the divine spirit of the universe. But, in truth, I am not even sure about humans and the soul, so how can I know about animals? Like most people, I flounder, not quite knowing but always hoping, and always yearning to shut down reason and look up to see dog shapes in the stars.

Profound consolation came from reading that so many

cultures have recognised the divine within animals, and realising that dogs especially have been credited with much power. Why did our First Friend (to use Rudyard Kipling's phrase) appear on so much Mayan pottery, belonging to a period starting around 200 AD? Even before that, why did so many tribes in South America (and in fact in many other places too) bury dogs with their dead? Across the globe people have believed that dogs would guide them to the afterlife, and different cultures (from the Greeks to the Zoroastrians) have placed dogs as guardians between worlds.

In ancient India, Mesopotamia, China, Mesoamerica and Egypt, people had deep ties with their dogs and this was also common in ancient Greece and Rome. Ancient Greeks thought of dogs as geniuses, possessing a certain elevated spirit. I understand Homer's story of the ancient dog Argos, who recognised his master Odysseus (aged and in disguise) after twenty long years away, and wagged his tail, then died happy to have seen him. Dogs remember. For thirteen years after the end of my first marriage Bonnie would rush ecstatically towards my former husband, when she saw him perhaps twice a year, and lick his face as if he were still her master.

With that capacity for love and loyalty comes the ability to feel genuine grief. In *The Iliad* Homer gives us one of the most moving descriptions of animals mourning, when the magnificent chariot horses Xanthus and Balius 'stood stock still and wept' because their master, the charioteer Patroclus, has been 'brought down in the dust'. The animals are whipped, to no avail; nor can they be coaxed to move. Instead they weep, wetting their long, trailing manes with tears 'flowing down from their eyes to drench the earth'. Today's animal behaviourists present incontrovertible evidence that animals display grief, but Homer knew it first. What's more, his noble horses, crying for grief outside the walls of Troy, turn out to be as divine as that faithful dog in the Mahabharata: 'immortal beasts who never age or die'.

The philosopher Plato referred to the dog as a 'lover of learning' and a 'beast worthy of wonder'. That man was wise. Another Greek, Diogenes of Sinope, loved the simplicity of the dog's life and encouraged human beings to emulate it. In modern Turkey there is a statue of him with a dog at his side. While there have been changes in the way other animals have been perceived through history, the dog has remained a constant companion, friend and protector – portrayed that way through the art and in the writings of many ancient cultures. The old claim that a dog is man's best friend is shown in literature and in history – but so many of us know it anyway.

To me, mourning my dog, all these stories suggested an innate need to show reverence to the animal which gave up its wild existence to share food and fire with humankind. In the most 'primitive' myths as well as the greatest literature we can trace an awareness that pre-dates Darwin – a sense hard-wired into the human psyche that we are intimately connected with other species *and* that they can be our guides. Holding that thought, if an animal has been seen as sacred and seen as having the power to guide humans, it seems to me this could not be the case unless the creature has a moral capacity. In other words, that the animal was seen as 'good'.

Of course, bad black dogs, devil dogs, also abound in folk tale and legend, but why wouldn't they? My tiny white dog is arm-wrestling with a black dog of gloom even as I write, and I know she will win that fight – because since she could always make me better when alive, so she continues that task now she is dead. Humans have always see-sawed between good and evil, struggling, succumbing, struggling some more … always hearing the good angels singing and the fallen angels yowling in hell and wondering which sound is the more seductive. That friendly stray dog might turn out to be the devil in disguise (as in Goethe's great work *Faust*) or lose his mangy hair shirt to shine before you as a holy being. Who knows? Better hedge your bets and be kind to animals…

ne grey day I arrived at the British Museum with an appointment to see Egyptologist Dr John Taylor. We met in the Great Court, the magnificent space (the largest covered courtyard in Europe) where it always feels that all resonances of footfall and voice combine in a soft, eerie thrumming, a cumulative din of whispers – as if all the dead (enshrined in thousands of objects within these walls) are speaking at once.

Dr Taylor took me to the Egyptian galleries upstairs, to contemplate a glass case containing animal mummies. Here we must start, with the reality of death and the difficulty of knowing exactly *why* the ancient Egyptians

carried out certain acts. For example, as we stood in front
of the case containing some of the more famous mummified cats, my natural conclusion was that these were
beloved pets, preserved in order to accompany their owners into the afterlife. But the sweet sentiment of the cat
lover was dispelled in a few moments, when Dr Taylor

explained that these (even that kitten) were not pets but temple offerings to the cat god Bastet.

'So you mean they were sacrificed?' I asked.

He nodded.

This is not really what I wanted to hear. On the other hand, since cats, birds, dogs, monkeys and even crocodiles were mummified as votive offerings to specific gods, this at least credits the poor creatures with a bit of clout. Millions of animal mummies have been found in Egypt, and at one point (in unenlightened times) they were even ground down to make fertiliser. The animals were offerings, or cult objects, but they were also pets, and it is of those that I wished to speak to Dr Taylor.

He pulled out book after book, his academic training unwilling to indulge me in my wish for proof that the Ancient Egyptians believed that their pets had an afterlife, but at the same time willing to offer little dog-biscuits of encouragement. He showed me a picture of the limestone sarcophagus of Tamyt (meaning 'female cat'), belonging to Prince Djehutymose and dating from about 1350 BC, found at Memphis, near Cairo. There is the royal cat in all her glory, wearing a fringed scarf (or is it just a necklace?) and standing before a pedestal table bearing a duck and some vegetables, in case she gets peckish on her journey to the next life. The four corners of this coffin bear the names of four holy beings who will act as her protectors and on the lid Tamyt calls on Nut, the sky god, wishing to become 'an imperishable star'.

Dr Taylor agreed that everything indicates that this was not a votive animal, but a beloved pet. I like to imagine beloved Tamyt, purring as she was pampered by her prince...

Hearing about the way the ancient Egyptians loved (yes, I will choose to use the non-academic word, although Dr Taylor was naturally cautious about it) their pets narrowed the gap of millennia that separates me from the women in the wall paintings at Luxor, their little dogs beneath their chairs. Egyptian art shows dogs, cats, falcons, monkeys, gazelles, ducks, baboons and other creatures alongside human beings, in a glorious land-scape of reeds and sunshine. Household monkeys wore bracelets, anklets and earrings, and dogs large and small were similarly adorned, the magnificent hunting hounds held on fine leashes. Dr Taylor showed me an image (in Patrick F. Houlihan's wonderful book *The Animal World of the Pharaohs*) of a stone relief found in a tomb at Saqqara. It shows a man feeding a flop-eared puppy with his mouth, both their tongues clearly visible. Is he attempting to wean the animal after the death of its mother? There's a jar being held out to him from one side; maybe it contains milk which he is warming in his own mouth to feed the rather piggy little puppy. Sitting inside an office in the hallowed walls of the British Museum I kept quiet about my guilty secret – that from time to time I would feed my own flop-eared little dog with my own mouth.

Everything has happened before. At some stage during the Middle Kingdom (from 2008–1630 BC) an Egyptian lady had a wooden coffin made for her beloved pet dog. The dog was small, but dearly valued – because on the coffin her mistress had carved the inscription: 'The loved one of her mistress, Aya.' Some people think the hieroglyphic for the name means 'Woofer'. Yes, that long-dead woman loved her lapdog, just as I do. In my imagination I hear her crooning endearments, petting her baby, telling her all the troubles of her world, and finding comfort...

Patrick Houlihan refers to a 'partnership' between the ancient Egyptians and animals: 'Both were created by the gods and both were the bearers of life. Therefore animals were entitled to love and care.' The high status of the dog in human affections was also indicated by a remark made by the Greek historian Herodotus, that 'when a dog also died in an Egyptian house, the family shaved the whole of their bodies' in mourning.

But did they believe that their pets had a soul? Dr Taylor pointed out that souls were weighed in the hall of judgment, 'and you never see images of animals there'. I suggested that maybe that is because the animals do not need to be judged, because they are innocent. He talked to me about Egyptian idea of the soul: the *ka* (vital force), the *ba* (individuality) and the *ankh* (what you become after death, presumably after judgment) and in the end we both shrugged, the academic and the writer forced to bow their heads before what cannot be known. Anyway, this rich subject is so vast and I had to leave for an appointment: I must make a lunch-time speech about my last book. I can't make a living from wondering whether my little dog had a soul, but I can certainly identify with Woofer's sad mistress.

Much later, back at home, I read an essay by the American scholar Edward Bleiberg:

The Ancient Egyptians … did not regard animals as inferior to humans. Not only were they not inferior, but also some animals … either were or contained a ba, a part of the soul that is active in this world and the spiritual world. They believed that animals have – or actually were – souls, whether alive or dead. Animals could also become gods, through death and mummification, just as humans could also become divine through the same sequence. Or more specifically, a deceased animal … could achieve immortality, also the hope for humans after death.

None of the Egyptians' neighbours in the Mediterranean believed this, Bleiberg notes: 'The view that animals were soul-less was passed from Judaism and the Greek and Roman world to Christianity and, ultimately, to modern Western cultures.' That may be true, but we do not have to believe it.

🐈 🐈 🐕 🐕

Some years ago the distinguished veterinarian Bruce Fogle conducted a survey into his British co-professionals' attitudes to pet death. He found that one out of five practising vets (subject to a long and rigorous scientific training, after all) believed that a dog has a soul and an afterlife. Interestingly, two out of five in that group believed the same of humans. But when the same survey questions were put to vets in Japan (where, we must remember, Buddhist and Shintoist traditions allow sanctity and an afterlife for all living things), every single vet surveyed stated a belief that dogs have a soul that survives death.

I wanted to discuss this with a local vet, but not one who had ever met Bonnie. So I was put in contact with Pippa Ashman, who came to my house and fussed over a delighted Sophie – approving the fact that we had chosen a rescue dog. Pippa chose her career when she was six, trained in Bristol and then joined the Royal Army Veterinary Corps for four years. For a while she had her own practice in Bath, but now works night shifts in Bristol for the People's Dispensary for Sick Animals. We talked for a while about the grief she has witnessed, professionally, when people experience the death of a much-loved pet.

Unfortunately vets can seem unfeeling because it is part
of our everyday life. But to the people it is a great shock;

*I've seen them become emotional wrecks. So as a vet you
have to see what they need and try to talk on their level.
For example, I might suggest that when they wrap the
animal in a blanket, the head is left out. Because then it
looks as if it's asleep, you see?*

Pippa emphasised that she is a dog lover as well as a
vet, and understands the grief, because she has experienced it herself and remembers how her own mother
suffered for 'at least five years' after losing her favourite
collie. Therefore she will be gentle with people's needs
and beliefs.

*Once a woman was crying hard because we'd had to put
her dog to sleep and I needed to comfort her, so I said, 'He
doesn't need his body on this earth any more.' She said,
'Yes, I know – I told him the other day that he was going
to join my mum in heaven. And in time I'll join them
both… but not too soon.' Then she gave a little smile at
her own joke, and I felt she was comforted by what she
believed – the idea of being in heaven with her mother and
her dog. In circumstances like that it's not my job to tell
anybody what I think, but to say what I think will make*

*them feel better. And if that means seeming to agree that
the pet might go to heaven, well…*

Yet Pippa Ashman does not believe anything of the kind.

*Honestly, I struggle with it. Why would you differentiate
one animal from another? What about a woodlouse? How
can heaven accommodate them all – and the dinosaurs
too? When people talk about a dog having a spirit I want
to know what form it takes. I have never seen a ghost of
anything, but I have friends who say they have – human
and animal, and those friends are much more intelligent
than I am. The human brain is such a powerful organ we
can imagine anything – like the sound of your dog in the
room after he has died. You know, I'm a vet and when I
try to go beyond my own experience, I struggle. But…*

She paused, then grinned. 'I admit I don't know.'

Sophie, our little rescue Chihuahua cross, has settled
peacefully on the sofa next to Pippa – which is something
Bonnie would never have done. Her place was right next
to me or on my lap, but Sophie is more relaxed. Noting
this, Pippa made a very interesting assertion. In all her

years as a vet, she said, she has noticed a clear difference 'between a dog that has known a period of suffering and one born with a silver spoon in its mouth. That's how I put it – meaning the dogs who have been bred in perfect circumstances then gone to an excellent home.'

So what is the difference?

The ones who have experienced ill-treatment or been abandoned or other hardship – they are the ones who are grateful. I've seen it time and time again. I always tell people that they will get a much better return on their love if they choose to rescue a dog. Those animals know that they have been rescued, got out of trouble – and they pay the debt back.

It seems to me that is a remarkably – and delightfully – non-scientific, non-professional remark to make. For to say a dog can feel 'gratitude' seems to imply a moral awareness in the animal – a sense of obligation to the human whom they recognise as a saviour. If a sensitive but matter-of-fact ex-Army vet says that she has observed 'gratitude' in dogs, then where does that feeling – or instinctive response – actually come from? Did Bonnie feel grateful to me because I was her rescuer, and is that sensation what Sophie is already experiencing – now that she knows this peaceful place is her 'forever home'?

Naturally, I have no difficulty in believing that. Gratitude is an acknowledgement of a benefit received and recognised as such and modern psychological thinking has identified it as vitally important to mental, physical and spiritual health. This awareness simply builds on what has been a core belief in the Christian, Buddhist, Muslim, Jewish, Baha'i and Hindu traditions. In the Orthodox, Catholic and Anglican Churches the most important rite is called the Eucharist – that name coming from the Greek word *eucharistia*, meaning 'thanksgiving'. In my advice column I have, from time to time, suggested to somebody in distress (often through loneliness or bereavement) that they try what is now a well-recognised therapy: keeping a 'gratitude journal'. Just writing down each day three things that made you feel thankful, no matter how small (the girl in the shop smiling at you, for example, or the sight of daffodils in the park), can heal the troubled soul.

A dog 'writes' its gratitude with every wag of the tail and when a cat climbs on to your lap to curl in a ball, making your whole body vibrate with its purring, that beautiful animal epitomises pure pleasure. And if pleasure is an essential part of gratitude, who is to say that the animal is *not* 'grateful' for human nurture, affection, love? Yet to use these 'human' words possibly sells the dog short. What if the animal is pure sensation, and that is their glory? Perhaps what we project upon them is what matters, and what they arouse within us is their greatest gift.

Therefore it need not matter to me whether Bonnie and now Sophie actually knew 'gratitude'. Naturally, I am prepared to imagine the animals have that spiritual dimension, but it hardly seems to matter any more. In a sudden epiphany (as the soft rain falls outside and I smile here at my desk because Sophie is snoring like a train and you could not believe such a tiny body could produce such a powerful noise) I understand that the essential element in the bond I had with Bonnie is the thankfulness I feel *myself*. So much has been written about animal–human relationships, so many experts have theorised about dogs, but now all that feels like so much (admittedly fascinating) noise. As noisy as this little personality snoring beside me – and as ultimately mysterious.

I glance down to the opposite side of my desk, where Bonnie's bed once stood – the place Sophie stared at so fixedly that day – and contemplate the wooden box placed there, the one containing Bonnie's relics. The time is now coming when I must dispose of the last of her ashes and when that moment comes it will be an act of reverence. Without knowing exactly what I mean, I feel that my soul will fly somewhere I cannot name – to meet hers.

Because loving an animal – *really* loving with humble gratitude – sets you in the way of grace. 🐾

CHAPTER TEN

But that free servitude still can pierce our hearts.
Our life is changed; their coming our beginning.

<small>FROM 'THE HORSES' BY EDWIN MUIR (1887–1959)</small>

1 May 2016

Last night I dreamed about Bonnie. Suddenly she was
there, curled at the foot of my side of the bed. In the
dream I reached and touched her, knowing quite well she
had died six months ago, and not daring to believe that I
could see her, curled in a ball, just like before. But I could
feel her silky coat and it was wonderful. She was warm;

I could see the slight rise and fall of her breathing, but could not wake her. My mother walked into the room and I told her Bonnie was there – really there – but she shook her head and could not, or would not, see her. Then Robin arrived, and I told him to look because she was there. His face was very sad and he shook his head, yet he did seem to be able to see something, there on the bed. Now I heard yapping outside the bedroom door. It was Sophie, begging to be let in. But I did not want her in the room. I wanted Bonnie to wake, needed to hold her again. So I reached out and stroked her sleeping head and felt her warmth and sighed her name. Then she was gone.

Vanished.

So I got to my feet and went to open the door and Sophie rushed into the room squealing with excitement. And I was glad.

THE DIARY ENTRY marks the final turning point. Dreams do that for us, the subconscious nudging us forward. Six months have passed since my dog died; this book has been a reaching out to those who know what it is to mourn a beloved animal, as well as (I hope) a conversation with those who find such sorrow impossible to comprehend, that they may now feel a twinge of doubt at the certainty that says, *Only a dog*. As I grow older I trust certainty less and less. The most beautiful skies can be grey, yet shimmer like mother-of-pearl, holding all the light we cannot see.

Perhaps the mission to explain becomes easier if we detach the love and the loss from its particular object. Were I writing about a 'real person' you would certainly understand, therefore let us pretend that is the case. Since the death of that small, furry white person I find myself changed to a degree I never expected, in body and spirit. Yes, all this time. Health is obvious, but the relentless, prickly sadness was barely noticed even by those who love me. Why should it be? Some things must remain concealed. Painful as it is to confess, without my friend I was brought low by what felt like existential loneliness; it seemed to me that nobody ever knew me like that one small creature knew me, in the darkness of the night. No human love (despite my many blessings) has given me such wordless understanding, such acceptance, such absolute devotion. No welcome was ever like hers and there are no words for how I miss that joy. Without her mute devotion and old energy beside me, something essential, some soul-spark, has sickened and flagged.

But it will come back. She – my muse and friend – tells me so, therefore I believe.

Those who have read Philip Pullman's great trilogy 'His Dark Materials' will be familiar with his extraordinary imaginative creation, the dæmon. This creature is the external physical manifestation of a person's inner self, changing its animal forms when a person is young, becoming fixed in a final shape at puberty. The dæmon possesses intelligence and speech; the spirit-creature and the person are one entity in two bodies and the greatest human agony is to be split off from your dæmon, losing your spiritual essence. Leonardo's *Lady with the Ermine* prefigures Pullman's heroine Lyra Belacqua and her dæmon, Pantalaimon, and when I first read *Northern Lights* I recognised this pair. About six years before Bonnie came into my life, they spoke to something deep within me. So when at last I met my little dog I was ready (thanks to a great writer) to recognise my witchy familiar, my soul-animal. But what if each one of us has a dæmon? Maybe people never realise they are accompanied by invisible animal-spirit companions and guides. But I feel blessed to have known.

Six months have gone since nature attempted to split us. Bonnie stopped being a part of the physical world but she became a part of everything else, including me. The great Parisian Anatole France (1844–1924) wrote: 'Until one has loved an animal a part of one's soul remains unawakened.' I resist proclaiming that too loudly because it expresses the unacceptable arrogance of the born-again animal lover. Who are we to lay claim to awakened souls and exclude the rest? Nevertheless I know exactly what he means. I also like another of France's dictums: 'If the path be beautiful let us not ask where it leads.' So all of us walk together...

During the writing of this memoir I researched mediums who claim to be able to contact dead animals, and animal 'whisperers', who believe they can tune into a living animal's 'speech' and interpret it. I read about a woman who says she can do it over the telephone. Really? Maybe I am truly lucky, because my dog communicated with me for sure and that is all I need to know.

Naturally I'm aware that such a blunt statement sets me firmly on a road towards belief. But belief in what? Although I would love to rest my faith in an afterlife where Bonnie bounds across the clouds to greet me,

I cannot. It is almost as if I am rejecting such an easy consolation, because it attempts to deny death, deny pain. When you commit to loving a special animal, you have to accept the pain of assuming that (in the natural order of events) it will die before you, leaving you changed equally by the love and the loss. This grief echoes and prefigures other sorrows you will inevitably endure in life – and accepting it is to embrace an essential part of the human condition. Thus you allow your love for the animal to lead you on, even if the pathway towards the spirit is full of stones. Or rather, *because* it is full of stones.

🐾 🐾 🐕 🐕

Once upon a time I sat in a very small plane looking down on the largest, most awe-inspiring landscape I had ever seen. It was 1997 and I had spent an extraordinary, memorable, week in Arnhem Land, the vast wilderness in Australia's Northern Territory, traditional home of the Yolngu people. Now it was time to return to Darwin, and on the way I was to experience one of those epiphanies you wait for all your life – described beautifully by Sylvia Plath as an angel flare, a trick of radiance, a 'rare, random descent'.

My head buzzed with wonders, like the aboriginal wall paintings we had trekked to in that wild, beautiful land-scape and the weathered skeletons 'buried' in those same caves in niches open to sun and wind. I had whispered to them, asking permission to be there. In the wilderness I felt moved to speak to every living thing I saw: the baby crocodile sunbathing on a rock, the rare, vivid orange Leichhardt's grasshopper, sea eagles whirling overhead, cockatoos, flying foxes, frilly lizards, frogs, yes, even the huge barramundi I caught, fishing (for the first time in my life) in the Cato River. The magnificent fish was cooked by a Yolngu family in their camp at Dhalyny-buy and tasted more delicious than anything I had ever eaten. But how important it was to thank it: the fish will feed you, therefore it requires honour. This seemed to me superior to the Christian saying of grace.

As we flew to Darwin I looked down at the vast shapes of rivers, streams, sand bars, rocks and forests, and clearly saw the spirit of my barramundi lying in the landscape. Suddenly they were all there in a vast pattern below me – the dancing outlines of the creatures and spirits painted in the old rock galleries and in aboriginal paintings on wood, and the living ones we had seen and heard in the wild. So the natural world and the imaginative world of art and mythology became one, spread out below in the new collective noun that flashed into my mind: a worship of animals. The glory of it dazzled me so much that when we landed I couldn't help blurting to our experienced ranger/ guide: 'I just saw all the animals drawn on the earth.'

Would the stalwart young rugby player, the epitome of fit Aussie masculinity, smile in gentle mockery at the fanciful Pommy Sheila? No. He nodded seriously and said, 'Yeah – I did too.'

Animistic beliefs that see everything as possessing a soul were common among our earliest ancestors. Every tree, every flower, every fish, every deer, every dog was 'en-souled', with feelings and purpose not entirely unlike our own. Fairy tales and myths of transformation are links to that 'primitive' past and no antipodean aboriginal or Native American or South American tribal elder would find it strange to hear direct spiritual communication in the eerie cries of dingo, loon or condor. When Wordsworth walked the hills and dales of the Lake District and the Quantocks the sublime poet of the Romantic imagination was permanently tuned in to the Great Spirit, the moral force of nature itself, which 'rolls through all things'.

There is nothing strange in such ideas; on the contrary, I have reached a point in my life where I find it weird that people do *not* understand them, because they have removed themselves so far from nature they lack all respect for its needs. Corrupted by the arrogance that caused the first fall, we have trashed the planet and cruelly ignored the dignity and rights of animals – and the gates of Paradise clang shut behind us.

(Since I have used the phrase 'rights of animals' I should explain here that the angry, ignorant political actions of the so-called animal rights movement have nothing to do with my idea of a teeming world of nature far more important than we are. 'Rescue' mink and unleash death into the wild... Oh, congratulations! Blinkered, hate-driven ideologues have even proclaimed that it is immoral to keep pets, which is the ultimate proof that they know nothing about the special relationship that informs this book, and motivates all those who work, the world over, for the welfare of animals.)

It would be such a useful exercise to spend half a day imagining that every living thing you see is possessed of

a spirit all of its own. So each humble clump of prim-
roses, each tree in the park, each regimented flower in
municipal beds, each squirrel, each dog on a lead trying
vainly to stop and sniff, each cow, each horse, each crow,
each cat, each rat and all the multifarious teeming life
of plants and animals the world over... Each would be
seen as a fellow spirit, rather than an inanimate *thing* out
there, to be ignored or exploited. Imagine. It would (in
George Eliot's words) 'be like hearing the grass grow and
the squirrel's heart beat, and we should die of that roar
which lies on the other side of silence'. It will not happen. No wonder the wise novelist added bleakly, 'As it is,
the quickest of us walk about well wadded with stupidity.'

When, earlier in this book, I talked about William
Blake's third stage of understanding, the higher innocence, this is the meaning I was striving for. It is an
understanding rooted in innocent delight, then tempered
by the darkest experiences of life, then at last synthesised
(the two states of innocence and experience) into joyful, imaginative power. This ultimate state is prepared
to leave reason aside and embrace belief – as implied by
Blake's own question: 'How do you know but ev'ry Bird
that cuts the airy way, is an immense world of delight,

clos'd by your senses five?' That is where I am trying to get to: the light I see in the distance, the soul of Blake's bird. It may seem far from one little white dog dying in a sad woman's arms, yet it is not. Here we have been led – and the stages of the journey still arouse in me a boundless curiosity: a dog waiting for the moment to die at home, the surprise of a picture in an old doll's house, a Labrador called Dotty offering comfort, a physical 'nudge' from an invisible dog, a dream, a picture that seems to move, the seemingly random arrival of a new dog...

How can I make sense of these things without wondering about the animal soul? And because I do not understand, *cannot* know, I am prepared to let imagination leap free. Gandhi's injunction that we must 'be the change you wish to see in the world' leads to fresh steps forward. Unknowingly educated by animals long ago, I was set on a new path by one dog. And now I know *that* is the change I wish to see in the world – the willingness to admit naked love and unadulterated joy and rejoice in the pure, mysterious spirit of it all, without embarrassment.

Anyway, 'dog' is 'God' in reverse.

Robin and I take Sophie for a walk in the local cemetery. It had been my intention to make a pilgrimage to the Cimetière des Chiens et Autres Animaux Domestiques near Paris, or at least to the old Hyde Park Pet Cemetery, where the first pet to be buried, in 1881, was a Maltese called Cherry. There are 300 small graves there, each one marked with a stone and a touching message. But, dogged by illness and the demands of a weekly column, elderly parents and grandchildren, I ran out of time. Not long after Bonnie died we visited a friend (an immensely intelligent and chic woman, the wife of a prominent politician and businessman) who showed me her private pet graveyard – the spot in her extensive garden where she has personally buried four beloved dogs, each with a natural boulder-stone to mark the grave. In cold sunlight, we stood still in front of the row, as I read:

KATIE

My faithful loving friend.

Always by my side.

Forever in my heart.

Died 31 December 2005

TOFFIE

Our most loving loyal & mischievous springer for fifteen
happy years.
Died 19 June 2013

———◆———

DEBSIE

Forever loving. Forever trusting.
Brave to the end. With us forever.
May 2004–March 2015

———◆———

CASSIUS

Son of Katie. 31 March 2002–17 November 2015.
I was your friend. Deep love endures. It's not the end.
I am forever yours.

It was intensely moving to see and I felt honoured by
the privilege. But now I choose the less romantic patch
for pets in Bath's burial ground as another place to
meditate about the way we love and mourn our companion animals.

The day is hot and sunny. Sophie scampers at Robin's
feet; they walk around while I study the graves. Why
are we here? For fellow feeling, I suppose – an emotion

that makes it natural for me to approach the solitary dark-haired woman in her thirties, kneeling with great absorption to tend a recent grave. She tells me that Pippin was a yellow Labrador who lived until eleven and a half, but died two months ago. 'We wanted to bury him to have somewhere to come and visit, but some people were surprised. Cremation's more usual now, isn't it.' Yes, I say, we cremated our dog. Their lovely big Pippin was put in a coffin (the cemetery rule) and buried, as all the family stood round, 'thinking our thoughts about him'. We chat about how the death of a pet tears a hole in the heart of the family, and all the while she is on her knees, busy with the trowel. 'I come here two or three times a week to look after him,' she says, tipping a bedding plant from the plastic pot, ready to set in the earth above the family dog – who is still just that.

But no one has been near the grave of another Bonnie for a very long time. This 'dear cocker spaniel and special friend' was born in 1988 and died in 2004. Equally neglected is the grave of Bertie, 'an amazing Beagle and special friend 1983–1999' – but who can expect to tend an animal burial site for ever? Or a human grave, for that matter? All these cats – Scrumpy, Tibbs, Tara,

Caspar, Paris, Kamika, Pundalik, Fudge and the rest –
were loved, and even the one called simply CAT was 'a
friend and companion of our heart'. From the simplest
weather-beaten headstones to the fine, elaborate graves
in black marble with portraits engraved in the stone,
the graves are touching, the inscriptions repeating over
and over what we know of the bond between human and
animal: 'Our special friend.' An elaborate marble heart
enfolds a coloured picture of a fluffy grey cat called Amy
Law (this one given a surname like any family member)
and the message 'Our precious angel in God's safekeep-
ing, loved forever, forgotten never – Mummy and Daddy'.
This beautiful creature died in 2005 but her plot is still
carefully tended, with netting supported on posts over
the whole grave, to keep off the birds. Which, given a
cat's natural predations, makes me smile.

Are all those mentions of 'Mummy and Daddy' sentimental? Well, maybe. But they only seem mawkish to the
unbeliever: if you believe their sincerity they are not ersatz
but real. What's more, they prove that you can love the
unlovable. One grave has three dancing rodents carved in
the marble – rats, I think, although the skill of the funerary mason was less than the affection of those who had this

message carved: 'You were with us such a short time but you will always be in our hearts – we love you.' Merrily my imagination conjures up a picture of 'beloved terrier' Ben starting a wild chase (joined by all the cats) in those animal Elysian Fields. No wonder *his* owners had 'Forever Happy' engraved on his stone. Because that's about the sum of it – gloriously uncomplicated to me, as I stand among these memorials to animals, the silence only broken by a stranger's trowel. To borrow the simple words the novelist and dog lover Meg Rosoff puts into the mouth of a key character (a vet, as it happens) in her tender and funny story 'Jonathan Unleashed' – 'Dogs tend naturally towards happiness. That's why humans choose to live with them.'

People love their animals (why should a rat not be loved?) and in a very short time they say goodbye and mourn them, and then it all moves on. But we are the better for it. While I am reading the small headstones Robin strolls with Sophie across beyond the plots into the space that awaits more of them – until he spots a fox in the hedgerow and decides it best to put her back on her lead. She may look like a hybrid fox cub but she's still small and vulnerable, and it's our new job to protect her. Each day it becomes easier to love her too.

Conversation:

B – *Do you think about Bonnie?*

R – *Yes.*

B – *In what way?*

R – *Things she used to do.*

B – *Does it make you sad?*

R – *Yes, always.*

B – *Even though we have another dog now?*

R – *Yes, because this dog isn't a replacement. They just
sort of run along beside each other. Imagine if you'd
had a lot of dogs in a life. You'd think of the whole
pack of them, running together...*

B – *Yes.*

D o animals have a soul? Do I have a soul? After so
much thought, I reach the conclusion that I simply
do not know, but if ignorance (or should that be innocence?) is good enough for the poets in my personal
pantheon, then it will be good enough for me too. I cannot be sure, yet I can hope.

Most people yearn for a 'somewhere over the rainbow' where 'troubles melt like lemon drops' – perhaps accessed by one of those special bridges guarded by dogs. Can we see that rainbow in this modern world of unbelief, when even fairy tales are out of fashion? That question is asked by the American psychologist Sheldon Cashdan, who adds, 'The fairy tale historian and social critic Marina Warner ... argues that fairy tales help us imagine another life. They allow us to tell alternative stories, to conjure up worlds where happy endings are possible ... [and] strike a chord of optimism that resonates deep in the hearts of all human beings.'

The belief in an afterlife for animal companions (and humans too, although that is not my subject) is an expression of that hope – far more than wishful thinking, but a direct connection to the collective unconscious that Jung identified as the soul of the world. Fantasy it may be, but how can that be proved? Neuroscience cannot yet explain how the imagination works, nor what invisible energies it generates. The French mystical writer Christian Bobin makes a liberating point about belief: 'God may be simply a matter of sensitivity, the finest of our nerve roots, a thread of gold a thousandth of a millimetre through. In some of us the thread is cut, in others the least thing sets it vibrating.'

For me 'the least thing' was the death of my dog. The high vibration of her dancing particles reminded me of what my first love (the one I was going to telephone in July 1966 when I found baby bird Fred) explained to me about quantum physics, fifty years ago, when we were earnest teenagers who read John Donne aloud instead of going to parties. My wholly unscientific soul was enthralled by the idea that everything is permanently in movement, that nothing is fixed. My understanding was that energy is not destroyed, but changes. I was recently pleased to read a blog by an American particle physicist, Sean M. Carroll, who wrote: 'Surely it's okay to take account of indirect evidence – namely compatibility of the idea that some form of our individual soul survives death with other things we know about how the world works.' He remains agnostic, of course, but at least he poses the question. And my own insatiable curiosity invites me to run with it.

If you try the graceful form of martial arts called t'ai chi, you gain valuable insight into energy. This is not some new-age shibboleth, but a wisdom shared by many cultures: *chi* or *qi* in China, *gi* in Korea, *ki* in Japan, *prana* in India, *pneuma* in ancient Greece, *ruah* in Hebrew culture, *mana* in Hawaii and so on. All recognise the power of vital energy, the active principle, the very breath of life. Is this what the ancient Egyptians meant by *ka*? Or would it be *ba* or *ankh*? Thinking of the ways my dog has reached me after death I am in a mood to accept the whole damn lot and tell her, 'May the force be with you.' Because I think it is.

If it is true (yes, yes, I deal in 'ifs') that energy cannot be destroyed, and if we believe that love is the greatest energy of all – the vital force within human beings and the great thrust of creation in the wider world – then can love be destroyed? For me Wordsworth's idea of the force that 'rolls through all things' is more than nature itself, but the divine spark of love. And I see no reason why the energy generated by reciprocal human–animal love should not be a living part of that whole, helping to maintain its great dynamism and balance. That is my definition of 'soul'.

(And what of the unloved ones? The beaten, starved, neglected animals who are victims of unspeakable cruelty? Their natural energy of love is not awakened, but gradually destroyed. As I become older I find myself angrier than ever on their behalf. But I do believe in karma – another hidden energy, the vast surge of universal justice we cannot see. The value of every human being can be weighed according to how they treat all things – human, plant and animal, young and old – who are weaker. We can only trust that those who betray that sacred duty will be punished in time – and I myself would show no mercy. There are plenty of places in hell.)

Asked whether I believe your companion animal, or mine, has a soul, I will turn the question aside by invoking St Francis and his animal brothers and sisters and telling the story of St Kevin. Christians can think what they will (and Christianity is my religion) but all that matters to me is the biblical injunction to be kind to animals – an instruction shared in Judaism and Buddhism too. St Kevin serves as an example. He was a sixth-century Irish saint, who was praying in a cell so small that one of his arms (raised wide to the heavens in worship) was forced to stretch out of the window opening. He was so rapt in prayer he did not notice the blackbird that alighted on his open hand, built a nest and laid an egg. Now the saint must wait, because he could not move and destroy the unhatched life. In Seamus Heaney's 1996 poem about this legend, the message is clear: St Kevin, 'finding himself linked | Into the network of eternal life, | Is moved to pity'.

The real focus of the story is an unhatched chick, a fragile creature for which the saint feels great tenderness. That nurturing love and faith links him (and us) directly to the larger 'network' but it does require endurance too. Everyone who has loved an animal knows that. To find meaning within the life and death of one beloved creature is to put your hand out of the window and wait patiently for the miracle to alight.

Inevitably, the great energy of love will, in time, weaken. Gradually people will cease to feel the presence of their loved ones, animal or human. The vibrations will gradually grow weaker, while some love remains (like the ashes I have left) but the rest moves on to another home. But yes, I am contented to name the energy itself 'soul' – and its sheer, shimmering beauty and power makes the thought of any afterlife redundant.

For everything is *now*.

S o what remains to be done? There are the last steps
to be taken.

One day, browsing online as one does without quite
knowing what marvels will come your way, I came across
an exquisite, handmade in fabric and wool, miniature
Maltese dog nestled in a neat carrier with a handle. She
(the Dutch maker specified this was a female dog) was
expensive, but had to be bought. When the parcel arrived
it felt as if Bonnie had come home. So I presented her to the
lady in our family doll's house: the doll mother is me,
the doll Maltese is Bonnie and we shall live there for

ever, making the doll family complete at last, as a small dog will. And just as another small dog did, giving me unexpected consolation when the woman who put her picture in a doll's house was long dead. So let it be with this one.

Then there is a last ritual to enact – one which will form a loop to my past, and another lost love. In our walled garden is a sculpted memorial to Tom, the baby who was stillborn at full term in 1975. When I wrote (in Chapter Two) that all I have of him is a poor, fuzzy ultrasound image, that is not quite true. There is another relic, carried with me since April 1984, when I finally decided to write to St Thomas' Hospital, London, to ask what had happened to him. (It seems incredible that I did not know, but those were unenlightened days.) After a while a short, typed answer came back from a Miss Johnson, 'Assistant Director of Nursing Services, Midwifery/Gynae.':

I do understand your need to know what happened to your stillborn son. I have consulted the records and find that he was cremated at Honor Oak Cemetery and that his ashes were scattered midst the rose bushes. I hope this will bring you some comfort.

For all these years I have appreciated that clumsily poetic word, 'midst'. At the time I kept thinking I should go and visit those rose bushes in the south London cemetery, but never did. So now we have planted eight white, highly fragrant standard roses ('Margaret Merril') in the formal beds all around my baby son's memorial, in honour of one not-so-fragrant white lapdog, whose own memorial is fixed to the wall nearby. My husband digs a small hole at the base of each one, and I start to divide between them the larger, remaining part of Bonnie's ashes. And it feels to me – as we both bend to our quiet task amid the vibrant, silky May greenness – that all the loves and the losses in my life have become one, intermingling and fusing for ever. As I reach the last rose, immediately in front of the summer house where Bonnie and I used to sit and read and snooze, a sudden impulse makes me moisten a finger, dip it in the ashes, and place those last atoms of my pet on my tongue. Surprised and moved, Robin follows suit, and then I tip the last ashes into the roots of the last rose.

This feels fitting. At her end she tasted my tears; now I receive her back into myself and make it a beginning.

I take Sophie into the summer house, my special

retreat, for the first time. Nobody has been there since last summer, when Bonnie lay sleeping in her special place on the seat cushions, invariably on my right-hand side. I lift Sophie on to that spot – and immediately she freezes. The next minute she marches quickly across my lap to the opposite side. Deliberately I put her back, but the response is the same. The little dog makes a swift judgement with her feet and flops down on my left side, as if relieved to be free of the presence of the other dog. This time I leave her be. There is room in this little wooden structure for three rather small females. We all can look out on the roses together.

Sophie has turned out to be very much my husband's dog. But no matter; together we will walk beneath the willows and beside the river. This city child has been transformed into a woman increasingly detached from social life. But the Canada geese calling overhead; the *chwrir* of a kingfisher's split-second dazzle, the judder of dragonflies; the deer who stroll through the garden to nibble flowers; the badgers and moles who dig up the tussocky expanse we call a lawn (and we don't mind); the foxes who menace our wandering hens; the squirrels who strip our walnut tree; the mallard pair who arrive at our kitchen door each spring, to be fed by hand, and who later introduce us to the ducklings who even follow their mother over my sandalled feet... I love them all. One night my husband may call me outside when he does his last patrol before bedtime, and show me otter heads glistening in torchlight. If we are lucky the barn owl we watched last year will nest in the bespoke box we have placed high on a tree, in welcome. Waiting for all these moments is an antidote to mortality. This is what the Pulitzer Prize-winning poet Mary Oliver meant when she wrote about taking your place in the family of things.

Bonnie is forever a part of this great joyful unity. She

is in the high whisper of the wind in the Scots pine. She inhabits the strange patch of rainbow above the valley, that phenomenon of light they call a sun-dog – a mysterious halo in the sky. But although the blue paperweight on my desk will always call me into her swirling spirit, it is time to focus on the flesh-and-blood dog, the funny little foxy waif who now trots, busy and loyal, at my heels, caressed with all the new, silly, loving names dogs need and deserve.

In time there may be more dogs, some of them soulguides too. Trust me, I'll be looking out for them every moment.

Waiting to be changed.

Now guide me out of the story, spirit;
I don't know where it is you lead, but I believe.

From 'The King of Fire Island' by Mark Doty (b. 1953)

ACKNOWLEDGEMENTS

M Y THANKS TO all the people who spoke to me who are credited in the text, and to my stalwart husband Robin Allison-Smith for his endlessly quiet, loving support, as well as the photographs.

I feel indebted to my publisher, Jeremy Robson, for suggesting this book and for his warm support.

It is not possible to give a comprehensive bibliography (because you absorb from so many places over years) but the following books have interested and inspired me, with a special mention for Mary Oliver, whose every word in poetry and prose informs my heart:

John Homans, *What's a Dog For?*

Konrad Lorenz, *Man Meets Dog*

Mark Doty, *Dog Years*

Lisa Tenzin-Dolma, *The Heartbeat at Your Feet*

Mary Midgley, *Animals and Why They Matter*

Jaromir Malek, *The Cat in Ancient Egypt*

The Brooklyn Museum, *Soulful Creatures*

Patrick F. Houlihan, *The Animal World of the Pharaohs*

Jessie Lendennie (ed.), *Dogs Singing*

I am grateful for the following permissions:

'Mercies' from *40 Sonnets* by Don Paterson, published by Faber (2016), reproduced by permission of the author c/o Rogers, Coleridge & White Ltd, 20 Powis Mews, London W11 1JN.

W. W. Norton for 'The House Dog's Grave' by Robinson Jeffers.

Extract from 'Her Grave' by Mary Oliver from *Dog Songs* (Penguin Books, 2013).

Extract from 'The King of Fire Island' by Mark Doty from *Deep Lane* (Cape Poetry 2015).

I tried to contact certain copyright holders but their failure to reply is not my fault and every attempt will be made in the future.